A Practical Guide To Curative Education

A Practical Guide To Curative Education

The Ladder of the Seven Life Processes

Robyn M. Brown

Lindisfarne | 2016

For Sunny who got me started, for Kathy who keeps me going, and for Clementine who has kept me company as I have written every word.

The publication of this work was made possible by a grant from the WALDORF CURRICULUM FUND

Published by Lindisfarne Books,
an imprint of Anthroposophic Press, Inc.
610 Main Street
Great Barrington, Massachusetts 01230

www.steinerbooks.org

Print ISBN: 978-1-58420-982-9
ebook ISBN: 978-1-58420-983-6

Printed in the USA

Contents

Preface

Karl König described the seven life processes not as *forms* in the sense of anatomy or physiology, but as a living and weaving etheric being.[*] He said the processes need to be taken as a whole, as something that lives and weaves: something that first establishes a rhythmical connection with the surrounding world (*breathing*); makes itself a "house" (*warming*); fills this "house" with substance (*nourishing*); breaks this substance down by its own effort (*secreting*); re-establishes it again in making it into its own substance (*maintaining*); *grows*; and *reproduces*. König describes these seven processes as forming a kind of ladder, in which each step must follow the other in this specific order. It's a sequence that must be maintained, he says, because the human being is an organism in process of becoming. Over the last few years I have been working with the seven life processes. I have noticed that they form a pathway that each child I have met through my work at Mulberry Farm has followed step for step in progressing through their own healing.

It's the same pathway I have found myself following as I have progressed from being a class teacher, frustrated by my lack of knowledge of how best to help the children I worked with who gave me concern, to someone striving to really work out of Rudolf Steiner's *Curative Education Course*.[†] In that course, Rudolf Steiner speaks of Curative Education as the deepening of Waldorf Education. The twelve lectures provide clear indications for working with the children who give us concern. For example, Steiner speaks there of the

---

[*] König gave three lectures under the title "The Seven Life Processes" in Aberdeen, Scotland in March 1960. These are available in Karl König, *A Living Physiology*, pp. 61-92 (n.p.: Camphill Books, 1999). Unless otherwise noted, allusions to König's lectures throughout the present work refer to these.

[†] Rudolf Steiner, *Education for Special Needs: The Curative Education Course* (London: Rudolf Steiner Press, 2014). Twelve lectures given in Dornach, Switzerland in June and July 1924 (CW 317). Referred to variously throughout as *Curative Education* (title of its first publication in English), the Curative Course, or *Curative Education Course*.

fundamental importance of learning to observe without judgment; he also gives pictures that can aid us in understanding the inner condition of children, as well as practical tools that we can implement. He describes movement work that can help children to heal; and he gives meditative direction for teachers, so that we can work on ourselves in order to better understand how to use these tools.

Many years ago, when I was first a class teacher, I would say that there were perhaps one or two students in each class that could have benefited from the work of Curative Education. Now I am often asked to observe classes. I would say that, on average, one-third of the children in each class I see could use this work; another third could use it to a lesser degree; and another third fit the pictures I was given to expect in my Waldorf teacher training thirty years ago. Teachers are looking for answers. Steiner has given us the answers. It's up to us to construct a new paradigm, one that takes up this deepening of Waldorf Education and uses it in the day-to-day work with the children in our care. Many of the old pictures are no longer useful, so we have to start fresh.

I have chosen to use the pictures of the seven life processes as a structure for this book because they form such a clear pathway for our progress. I have tried to present the contents of Steiner's *Curative Education Course* in a practical and thematic way, based on my own work and understanding. When I first saw Curative Education being practiced at Somerset School and Farm, working with Sunny Baldwin, I finally saw an approach that brought the children to a new place. Nothing I had observed during my time as a class teacher had ever made such an impact. The children might have come to Somerset with difficulties, but many of them were able to graduate and rejoin a "big class" without those difficulties. This is why I love the work. Rudolf Steiner has given us a huge gift and it's our job to take it up. If my experience can help one teacher or parent to have the courage to try something new then the purpose of this book will have been met. Thank you.

Robyn M. Brown
Mulberry Farm, 2015

1. BREATHING

Imagine a classroom before the children have arrived for the day. It's a Waldorf classroom, so the walls are soft pastel, painted in a way that seems as if your eye can see right into the color. The desks and chairs are made of wood. There is a beautiful chalkboard drawing on the board. The children's paintings are on the wall. Even though they all had the same theme, you can see each child's individuality shining through. It's also clear who struggled with their brush or the spacing on the page more than most of their classmates. The children's coats are hanging on hooks along one wall. Some of them have fallen off, and are heaped on the floor. Or maybe they just never made it to the hook in the first place. As you peek into the children's desks you see that some of them have ordered their things very neatly. And some of them look like they have experienced a small explosion. Some chairs are tucked-in just right, and some are not. One child has left his crayons in a heap on his desk, with one or two lying on the floor. The classroom is lovely and soothing, but there are a few discordant elements. A lamp shade is eschew. A curtain rod has come out of its hanger and hangs at an angle. The books on the shelf have been stuffed in helter-skelter.

Imagine the teacher. She is a good teacher; this is her second time through the grades. The chalkboard drawing on the board is her work. Secretly, many of her colleagues are jealous of her skill. She's also an excellent musician. Each of her lessons is meticulously prepared, but that preparation is wearing on her. Last night she didn't start her prep time until after ten. She was at school late. As usual. There is a crisis in the third grade, a teacher has quit and no one knows where he or she will find a replacement, but they have to find one fast. Someone has to meet with the parents to reassure him or her. Meanwhile, everyone will take up a little of that teacher's work and try to keep an extra eye out for that class. The teacher's own children have already had their dinner before she makes it home. Her husband is a really good man, supportive of her job, but no one wants to feel like a single parent forever and she wonders just how long he will continue to be so patient. Dinner was later than usual, so her children are late going to bed. This makes the teacher feel even more guilty, because isn't she always harping to the parents in her class about the importance of rhythm? By the time she gets her children in bed, she has almost forgotten that she hasn't eaten anything since breakfast. Her lunchtime was spent sorting out a problem with a four square game. So now she pours herself a bowl of cereal and sits by her husband in the living room. It's almost a relief to hear about his challenges during his day. It reminds her there is life outside of Waldorf Schools. She rinses her cereal bowl and leaves it in the sink with the rest of the evening's dishes. She will try to get them in the dishwasher in the morning. Her husband is worn out and heads for bed. She heads for her book bag and begins to memorize tomorrow's story. It will be well past midnight when she finally goes to bed.

Now her new day is beginning. She got up extra early to tidy the kitchen and pack lunches. She's working on her third cup of coffee. As she enters her quiet classroom she's grateful. It's the only time this room will be truly at peace all day. She sips her coffee and goes over her lesson plan one more time. She walks around the room and straightens up a few chairs. She sees the pile of crayons left out on Jasper's desk. She puts them all back in their case and then notices that all his colored pencils are scattered throughout his desk. It's impossible to find them without emptying everything out. She has to sort through too many crumpled up pieces of drawing paper to find them. What should have been practice pages are covered with stick figures shooting each other. She finds some of the pencils, but many are missing. Many of the ones she does find are broken and have teeth marks all over them. More that a few have been sharpened down to nubs. She also finds several paper airplanes stuffed into the mess. Looking around the room from her vantage point kneeling by Jasper's desk she sees the rest of the air patrol poking out of three other children's desks. That would explain the streaks of white she thought she saw out of the corner of her eye as she was writing things on the board yesterday. She does her best to bring a little order to this boy's chaos. She collects the airplane as well as the others in the other desks. She realizes she should take a look at her classroom from the rearview more often. She's been wondering what Max had been finding so interesting lately, and now she sees he's created a whole menagerie of creatures out of beeswax, erasers, and push pins. So that's what's happened to all the push pins! Then she moves on to the coat rack. She picks up the coats that are on the floor and hangs them on the hooks. Under Alice's coat she finds yesterday's homework. Another day Alice won't have her work to turn in, and she's already so far behind it's hard to imagine how she will ever catch up. The first of the children will begin to show up on the playground in a few minutes.

The teacher starts to feel a knot beginning in her stomach. She's a seasoned teacher, a respected teacher. When she started with her class in first grade the parents were very enthusiastic about her. She felt their admiration and support for the first year or two, but now there is something new in the air. They gather at the edge of the playground in the morning. Even from a distance she can feel that what they are talking about isn't good. There have been some complaints to the faculty chair. The teacher has received some disturbing e-mails, and at the last parent evening there were several pointed comments about her classroom management. One angry mother went as far as to suggest that certain children be asked to leave. No one mentioned names, but the whole group became very uncomfortable. Jasper's mother started to cry, but she was sitting way in the back and no one seemed to notice. She wasn't the only parent in the class who felt the remarks had been personal.

The teacher knows things aren't going as well as they could be. In her last class she had one or two children who she found challenging, but on the whole things had gone well. She had felt that her class was with her. But this class is another experience. There are just so many that she truly does not know what to do with. She's been afraid to say this out loud to any of her colleagues, but there are times every day where she feels she has lost the class. They are out of her control, and everything that used to work isn't working anymore. Many of the children in her class have come to child study, and she has passed on the suggestions the faculty made to the parents. Children have gone for various assessments. Some have come back with recommendations for special classroom equipment, or some guidelines about how their disabilities could be met in the classroom. The language used in the reports has made the teacher feel rather inadequate. She is unfamiliar with the disabilities the assessments have described, and feels she is in over her head with those labels. She was never taught how to work with children with these kinds of difficulties in her training. Some of the children are working with different therapists after school or are being pulled out of class during the day for some kind of extra support. Some are on special diets. Although the teacher can't say any of the children have gotten worse through this process, she can't say they have gotten much better either. With each new intervention there was maybe a short time where it looked like things were getting better, but on the whole, long term, there really haven't been any changes.

Outside the classroom three backpacks slam into the wall. The children are arriving. The school day is almost ready to start. Already the teacher feels she can't really breathe.

Imagine some children. Jasper is on the lawn outside his classroom door spinning in circles. And he's yelling a strange syllable that sounds like boop! Boop! Boop! Some of the girls are standing nearby watching him. They have a rather superior smirk on their faces. They think Jasper is weird. Some of the boys run into Jasper's orbit and begin to body slam him. He slams them right back. Now they're all yelling different syllables and spinning and slamming. They are laughing, but somehow it doesn't feel like they are having a good time. The closer it gets to the time the bell will ring, the more frantic the boys become.

At the edge of the playground some parents have gathered. They are watching the shenanigans but they are not amused. One little girl is clinging to her mother. Her name is Sienna and she is in Jasper's class. Her mother is patting her and asking her if she is afraid of Jasper and his friends. Sienna begins to cry and starts to suck on her sleeve. "I don't want to go to school," she starts to wail, "I want to stay home with you mommy! It's too hard and it's too loud in there. I can't do anything and I'm just stupid!" Her mother keeps patting and keeps asking her questions. What is too hard? Does her teacher help her? What does her teacher do about all the noise in the classroom? She asks her daughter if her tummy hurts. Sienna covers her belly with her hands and curls up on the ground. She's crying too hard to answer. Her mother picks her up and cuddles her next to her. The other parents cluck in sympathy.

Allen walks up to the group of parents. He has a very solemn expression, and begins in a somber voice to tell each parent their name, phone number, address, and the names of all their children, what grades they are in and who their class teacher is. The parents don't really know what to say. One of them praises him for his memory. Allen says thank you and walks away.

Max is over by the swings. He has brought a wrench to school with him and he's busily taking the swings down. He drops the bolts and the washers and the nuts into the sand. It will be a long time before anyone finds all of them again. He grabs the swings, one in each hand, and begins to run wildly around the playground with them.

Alice is sitting on the bench outside the classroom door. Some of the other children are sitting near her and they are talking about the homework from last night. One of them pulls out her spelling folder and begins to read the sentences she wrote out loud. Alice thinks about homework. She wonders what happened to her folder. She thinks she may have taken it out of her desk, but she can't really remember what happened to it after that. She will not have her homework to turn in today. She doesn't have her homework to turn in most days. Oh well. Alice doesn't feel that upset about it

Peter's mother is walking him up to the classroom. She is holding his hand, and carrying his backpack with her other hand. When she gets to the classroom door she sets the backpack down momentarily and buttons Peter's sweater for him. She notices his shoes have come untied and so she bends over and ties them for him. As she is doing this, Peter is looking around with a large grin. He greets each of the children he sees by name. Some of them respond.

The bell rings and most of the children line up. The teacher opens the classroom door and comes out to greet her class. Peter's mom steps him up to the front of the line. Before the teacher can greet Peter his mother begins to tell the teacher about his restless night. She doesn't really lower her voice, so many of the children hear this exchange. To their credit they try hard not to giggle. "Shake your teacher's hand, Petey," she says, and then she takes him into the classroom, takes off his coat, and hangs it and his backpack on his hook. Then she leads him to his desk, gives him a loud kiss and a hug and finally leaves him alone. The teacher is outside greeting the rest of her class. She makes sure each one pauses and looks her in the eyes. She loves this part of the day. In that little second she sees what each child might be able to become, what she loves about each one of them. If she only knew how to get them there.

Jasper has stopped spinning and has gotten a little closer to the classroom door. He's not really in line though. He bends over and puts one of his hands on the ground. His other hand is swinging in front of him. He's hoping he looks like an elephant. He points his bottom in the air and begins to make loud farting noises. "I'm an elephant," he announces, "A farting elephant!" Several of the children at the end of the line start to imitate him. Many of the rest turn around and start to laugh. The teacher does her best to ignore them, trying to keep her focus on the child who is right in front of her, with her hand out.

Sienna's mother has walked her up to the classroom door too. When they are close to the front of the line Sienna's mother begins a daily ritual. She kisses Sienna on each cheek and on her forehead and on her nose. "It's time to go in now SiSi. Give mommy a kiss and let go now. Do you think you'll be OK?" The mother turns to the teacher and begins to talk about Sienna as if she is not really there. "She's having a bad morning. She didn't want to come to school today, and it was really hard to get her out of bed this morning. Her bed was wet again." This last part the mother whispers, but not quietly enough that all the children nearby can hear her. Two of the girls look at each other and roll their eyes. They look at Sienna and snicker. "SiSi's tummy is hurting again. I put some tea bags in her backpack. Will you make sure she gets a cup of tea at snack?" The teacher smiles at Sienna's mother as kindly as she can, but she isn't really feeling all that kind. She takes Sienna's hand and gives it a little squeeze. Sienna doesn't look at her. She doesn't return the teacher's greeting. She is still sucking on her sleeve. She does enter the classroom and slithers around the side as close to the wall as she can get. She collapses in her seat and hides her head in her arms. She wraps her legs around the legs of her chair and starts to rock herself gently.

No one would know it to look at him, but Jasper actually has a lot of thoughts about starting a new school day. He does not want to go in that classroom. He does not want to spend yet another day facing up to things he can't do. It makes him so mad. How come everyone else can do things and he can't? How come he is so stupid? He hates singing and he hates his flute and he hates handwork and he hates his Main Lesson Book. It doesn't seem to matter how hard he tries to do those things. He can't do them and he hates them. And he still has to go in that dumb classroom. His teacher comes up to him. "Let me see that trunk Jasper," she says. "Now it's time to turn this back into a hand and let me give that good hand a shake. Let's go inside. Today will be a better day." Jasper thinks she is nice to say so, but he doesn't think he will have a better day. The day hasn't really started yet and already he feels like he can't breathe.

Jasper's mother has been watching all of this from as far away as she can be and still see what is going on. She doesn't want those other parents to see her. She knows what they think of her son. She is pretty sure that before much time has passed Jasper will be sitting outside the classroom door. He may end up in the office. She may get a call to come get him. She sees how kindly his teacher tries to greet him, and she feels grateful for that. But she wishes the teacher would figure out how to work with him better. It's just not right that Jasper gets sent out so much. Not that Jasper is easy. This morning he punched his little brother because his little brother got to the sink faster to brush teeth. He broke his cereal bowl because he slammed it too hard into the sink. When she asked him to be more careful he told her to go screw herself. She knows she shouldn't let him talk to her that way, but truthfully she is a little afraid of him. More than once this year he has hit her. Hard. He gets really mad and she can't calm him down. She is afraid that someday he will really hurt her. She turns away and walks back to her car. Maybe today the school won't call. Maybe she will have these few hours while the boys are in school to breathe a little bit.

The teacher shakes what she thinks is the last hand of the morning. Already there are complaints about Jasper. Jasper hit. Jasper pushed. Jasper stepped on my lunch. Can't Jasper get in the classroom door and over to his seat without tromping on someone or something? Apparently not. She goes to the front of her room and stands as tall as she can. She sighs deeply and tries to feel where her feet are. It used to be that all she needed to do to bring her class together was stand like she is trying to do now and wait quietly. The class would fall right in with her. But this group does not fall in. Some do. Some of the children are standing and waiting patiently. Some of them are losing patience and are swirling around giving the disruptive ones the stink eye. It doesn't help. Jasper has collapsed on top of his desk, feet, legs, hands and arms waving in the air and rubbing his back on his desk like a bear with an itch. The children around him are laughing encouragingly. One last paper airplane the teacher didn't happen to find while she was inspecting desks this morning sails through the air. It lands on Sienna's head. She bolts upright from her little heap and screams as if she's been scalped. The teacher tries the one trick that sometimes works. She starts to count. It's early in the day and the class cuts her some slack. By ten they are reasonably quiet. She's just about to start Morning Verse when in gallops Max. He has the chains of one of the swings he took down slung over each shoulder, and his backpack is balanced precariously in the swing's green plastic seat resting against his back. He neighs loudly and skids to a halt. The classroom explodes. Even Sienna smiles. The teacher just stares at Max, not sure how to react. "What!" Max demands. "What indeed," says the teacher. "I'm just bringing in my backpack," says Max. "And you need special equipment to do that?" says the teacher. She hopes the sarcasm isn't too pointed in her voice. "It's my wagon," says Max seemingly innocently. "I can't haul my goods to town without my wagon." "The wagon goes back outside," says the teacher. "We'll have to figure out how to turn it back into a swing later on. But right now you are late. By five. Everybody ready." And by five, miraculously most of them are. Or close to it. If you don't count Allen who is trying to straighten out the kinks in the paper airplane that crash-landed on Sienna. Or notice that Max is standing on one leg and leaning hard on his desk. Or that Alice is staring out the window and not likely to join in the verse. Neither is Sienna for that matter. She's curled back into her heap on her desk. Peter will turn around and face the class during verse. He won't join in, but he'll grin hugely. He seems to feel they are reciting it just for him. No one expects that he will participate. Jasper is whispering "fart, fart, fart." But at least he is truly whispering, and for now no one is paying attention. Somewhere the teacher knows she should wait for all of them to be ready to join her, but by now she is happy to just have most of them ready. She doesn't wait for the rest. She starts the verse. The day gets worse from there.

During the singing only some of the children are singing with her. It's a beautiful song and the teacher sings it beautifully. Her last class loved it, but in this class there just seems to be too many that can't follow the tune. Or they don't have a feeling for the rhythm. Many of them seem to think the point of singing a song is to get to the end first. First one done wins! So no matter how hard she works at it the teacher can't seem to get them to sing together. Jasper is singing loudly in a falsetto. He adds little embellishments to the end of each line. Unfortunately you can hear him better than anyone else in the class. Some of the children aren't singing at all. They have turned to watch Jasper. One girl lifts her arms and begins to "conduct" him. Jasper shows his appreciation by singing even louder. Max has his hands in his desk again. Probably working on some new creation. Sienna has her forehead pressed to her desk and her hands over her ears. Alice is looking placidly out the window. At least nothing seems to disturb that child. Peter is humming a very nice little melody, but it is not the melody that the others are singing.

Things don't improve when the teacher asks them to get out their recorders. Although the majority of the class seems to be aware that a recorder is an instrument and meant to make music with, there are just too many that are using them for anything but music. Some point them at their neighbors and make gun-shooting sounds. Or they whack each other with them or use them as swords. Max has made a little ball of paper and is using his recorder to bat the ball across his desk. His desk mate tries to ignore him, but after awhile it's just too tempting. They get a proper game of desk hockey going.

All the morning circle activities follow along with the same theme. The teacher tries to get them to walk and clap out the sevens times table. Jasper stomps on the heels of the person in front of him, who starts to yell. Alice is moving forward, but her feet are not in rhythm and she doesn't attempt to clap. Her mouth isn't moving either. Sienna has moved to the very back of the room. She's sitting on the counter by the sink, sucking her hair. Peter isn't marching; he's jumping on two feet. His feet aren't in sync though and he's pretty wobbly. He's not saying the times table. It sounds like he's saying something like "plop" with each stilted jump. Max has added a rap bass accompaniment to the beat of the times table. It's not an improvement.

Finally it's time for the children to get out their Main Lesson Books. The teacher has written a lovely paragraph based on yesterday's material on the board. She asks the children to get out their Main Lesson Books and copy the paragraph into their books. When they have finished that they can start putting the drawing she has made into their books as well. It takes a long time for the children to settle. Some are quick to get out their work, but others find things to do on their way to pick up their books from out of the cupboard. Hands start to shoot up from children needing help. A lot of their questions they could answer just fine if they thought about it a moment, but they are used to asking assistance every little step of the way.

The teacher goes from desk to desk trying to get to everyone. The children who have raised their hands and are waiting for her start to fidget and talk to their neighbors. Peter's aid has arrived. She gets his Main Lesson Book out for him and opens it to the appropriate page. She gets out his colored pencils and puts a special device on his hand that will help him to properly grip the pencil. She takes his hand in her hand and moves it for him over the page, helping him to form the words the teacher has written on the board. Peter tolerates this with good humor, but his eyes are never on his work. He allows his aid to do what she will with his hand, but his attention is on the other children. He's watching what they are doing when the teacher's back is turned and he finds it very funny.

Some of the children work diligently, but as the work time goes by and the noise level goes up almost of the children become distracted. Sienna makes a little cave out of her head and arm and does her work all tucked into it. She writes the letters as small as she can, and very lightly, almost impossible to read. Several of her letters are backward.

Alice gets out her ruler and marks off a border on her page. Then she gets so involved filling curlicues into her border that she never gets to the writing. Max reads what is on the board out loud. Then he begins a monologue of disconnected thoughts, all of them slightly relevant to the subject matter, but not by very much. His writing is large and sloppy. Although he should be writing in cursive, he prefers a mixture of upper and lower case printing that doesn't follow any rules of capitalization found in any grammar book. He thinks what is written on the board is boring, so he is filling in with his own ideas, but he can't seem to get to the end of any one thought. He writes two or three long disjointed sentences, and then puts his Main Lesson Book away. He has yet to ever complete a page in his Main Lesson Book. He gets a reading book out of his desk and starts reading. His foot is tapping incessantly, but for now his mouth is still.

In the middle of the work time Allen starts to laugh. It doesn't really sound like a laugh, but it is. It's a rough guffaw kind of sound. Then he starts retelling a story. It's not a story from the curriculum; it's a story about a cat. One day a cat wandered into the classroom. It happened several years ago, but for Allen it's as if it just happened. The cat wandered into the classroom. It jumped onto the teacher's desk and fell asleep. That's it. That's the whole story. Allen has been telling and retelling this same story for years. He can't seem to get it out of his head. He looks around and realizes that the others are working in their books. He stands up to go get his. As he passes through the room he takes an interesting route. He could just curve around his desk and head for the cupboard where the books are kept, but Allen can't seem to move in curves. Instead he plots out a much longer route that is made up completely of straight lines and angles. As he turns at each angle he gives that spot a tap with his finger. Some of the children stop to watch him. Allen always moves this way. He moves in straight lines, and when he draws in his Main Lesson Book all of his drawings are only straight lines too. People's heads are squares and their bodies are rectangles. Allen rarely talks to the other children, but when he does it is to tell them the number on the license plate of the car they rode in that morning. Some of the children think that Allen is weird.

Jasper gets out his book, and for a while he tries. He really does try. He looks at the board and he sees what he should be writing, but when he looks away to try to write what he has just seen in his book he can't seem to remember what it was he was supposed to write. He repeats this process several times. He finally does get some of the sentences into his book, but when he looks at his work he thinks that some of his letters look stupid. He goes over them with his colored pencil. He goes over them again and again, but it doesn't get better, only worse. He hates how stupid he is. He hates how stupid his work looks. He gets out a black colored pencil and slashes the page with heavy black slashes. He's done trying to do this stupid work today. He looks up and happens to catch the teacher's eye. He looks so sad. He looks as if he just might cry. She starts to cross the room to come help him, but he jumps out of his seat before she can get there. He hurls his Main Lesson Book across the room and throws his desk over, spilling everything across the floor. He picks up his chair and throws it too. He turns so that he won't hit anyone with the chair, but he throws it.

The little moment of softness the teacher felt for Jasper is over. She tells him to head to the office. She will ask the office manager to call his mother to come and get him when she has a second at recess. Jasper's mother won't have much time to breathe today.

The teacher stands up Jasper's desk and puts his belongings back into it. She takes his Main Lesson Book back to the cupboard. By now, every time she turns her back she hears little disturbances behind her. If she only knew. Some children are crawling around on the floor. Almost all of them are talking and giggling. The paper airplanes are back. Sienna has wet herself. Her desk mate is staring at the puddle wondering what to do. Some of the children are still trying to work, but a lot of them are rocking in their chairs. Some of them are working with their legs wrapped around the sides of their chairs. They have pushed their work far to the side of their desk, and are twisted in their seats trying to see what their hands are doing. If you were to walk through the room you would see lots of pages where the writing looks like it's slanting off the page. You would see pages where it doesn't seem the child knew how to center the work properly. There are many crossed out words, and backward letters. Much of the handwriting is illegible.

By the end of the "quiet" working time the noise level has gotten so high the children can't hear the teacher when she tells them it is time to put their work away. She finally has to raise her voice to get them to be quiet enough to hear her. She's yelled at them and she hates that. It takes a very long time to get everything put away, but finally it is. Peter's aid packs up his work and puts it away for him. She gives the teacher a little sympathetic wave on her way out. Now it is time for story. This is the best time of Main Lesson. They all like story. Maybe Max won't feel as obligated to interject his thoughts into the narrative so much today. The teacher lights the candle and turns off the overhead lighting. She begins to tell her tale. Today even Max is absorbed. The children finally come to peace. The teacher finishes the story and Main Lesson is over.

The day doesn't get better.

As the last child leaves at the end of the day the teacher is left with a head full of complaints from the Special Subject teachers. They don't know what to do with Peter. Without his aid in the room there is no one to sit with him and help him with his work. When he gets bored he gets up and goes to the back of the room where he begins a conversation with an imaginary friend. Alice seems like she is catching on, but then she is never able to engage with her work, and so nothing is ever accomplished. At least she is quiet and sweet. Sienna fusses over everything, insisting she can't do it unless a teacher is right next to her more or less doing it for her. There are always a lot of tears involved. Allen is his own little mystery. No one seems to know what to do with him. Then there's Jasper and Max. Whatever progress the teachers feel they might be able to make seems to be completely undone by those two boys.

Once they start the rest join in and it's mayhem for the rest of the hour.

The teacher doesn't have any answers for them. She doesn't have answers for herself. She thinks about all the different reports and assessments she has read over the last few years involving these children. She has been introduced to words she never heard during her teacher training: ADD and ADHD; Spectrum disorders; Auditory processing disorders; Dyslexia; OCD; Sensory integration disorders; Developmentally delayed. She doesn't know what to do with these words. She feels she is out of her league. She doesn't have a special education credential. Maybe she should go and get one? But she's a Waldorf teacher and so much of what she hears from the experts about these difficulties just feels wrong. When she looks in the eyes of each of the children she doesn't see labels. In each of her children she sees something wonderful. She sees golden potential in each one, but at this moment that feels like sentimental nonsense. What good does it do her to see something wonderful in these children when she obviously can't reach those wonderful things? All those labels feel like walls separating her from the children. When she reads the reports she feels like she will never be able to understand how to give them what they need. It makes her feel like they are something separate from her. Something mysterious or foreign, but not in a good way; in a way that seems they will always be incompressible. She is at a loss.

She faces another evening of writing e-mails to the parents of these children. She tries hard to phrase her words positively, but it's hard to sound positive when she really feels so hopeless. The parents can read through the lines. Their children aren't learning. They are checked out. They are making it hard for the other children to learn. The parents know that they are being told that something is wrong with their child. They have all been doing their very best to do everything that the school has suggested. They have paid for expensive assessments, purchased special classroom equipment, turned their kitchens inside out to cook their children special diets and taken their children to every kind of therapy imaginable, but nothing is really improving. The parents are more than discouraged. Many of them brought their children to a Waldorf School because there the child was supposed to be respected as an individual. They were hoping that the teachers there would see the things that they saw in their children, but in reality it feels the same as it did in the places they moved to the Waldorf School to get away from. They want more for their children than just to be perceived as something that is not quite right. They want their children to flourish, not labor under a label and constantly feel singled out. They feel that their children are not being met in the Waldorf School. They are right.

In Karl König's first lecture on the seven life processes he describes breathing as "the establishment of an umbilical cord between the world and the living being." He says that without this life is not possible.

> Breathing, through respiration, takes in and breathes out the air which binds our ether body to our surroundings. The "mother" of our living body is in the atmosphere around us, and to this "mother" our ether body is connected by inhaling and exhaling; by this umbilical cord of air and *pneuma* or spirit. This is what is meant by *Atmung*. [The German word for breathing or respiration.]

Of course this can be understood literally, but we also have to look at it pictorially. As we take in sense perceptions, we are "breathing" with the world. We take in impressions, and breathe them into ourselves where they become memory. In this way breathing can be looked at as connected to our sense of touch, the ability to interface and connect with the world; to "touch" the world through all of our senses. Every time we want to become "alive" to something new, to grow or come to a new place of understanding we get there by following the path of the seven life processes. We have to start by "breathing." König says:

> Breathing is naturally the first of the seven life processes. It is the first because in breathing we communicate with the world. It is essentially what we call 'rhythm'; the giving and taking and the coming and going that connects us like an umbilical cord to the world. There is not something outside and something else inside, like two separate entities, which communicate with one another, but both are inside as well

as outside. It is living, it 'breathes' in the arms of the world, however it is not the breathing of air, but the rhythmical coming and going which is the important thing here.

It is just this kind of "breathing" that has been lost to us as we struggle to understand and work with the children we care so much about, but who remain a mystery to us; the ones that give us so much concern. We have somehow gotten off track, and so we have to begin again somehow. We have to begin by learning to breathe. We have to find the place where we know the innermost part of ourselves is connected to the outermost part of the world around us. We can breathe with it in a living rhythm that allows us and the world to become united. We have allowed the "science" of understanding children to separate us from the children right in front of us, and that has created fear and uncertainty. This fear is stopping us from breathing. König tells us that "'ensouled' breathing is percept making." As one of the first three life processes it is connected to thinking. When we are in a place where we can't "breathe" we can't form a real percept. Our fear causes our breathing to become "consumptive." Rudolf Steiner describes how at a certain moment in evolution the seven life processes succumbed to Ahrimanic and Luciferic influences. The first three life processes came under the influence of Ahriman. This is what caused "breathing" to fall under the danger of becoming consumptive, to become something merely material.

So where do we look to learn to breathe? After a long week with her class the teacher looks forward to the weekend. She looks forward to having some time to regroup. She knows that even though she is doing her best, it isn't good enough. Somewhere there must be an answer, she just hasn't found it yet. On Saturday afternoon the teacher has an hour or two to herself. Her husband has taken the children out for a hike, and the house is quiet. She counts on this little island of quiet each week to think about the week to come, to prepare new lessons, and try to find some new enthusiasm for Monday morning. She makes herself a cup of tea and heads for her study. She settles into a comfortable chair and takes up the book she has been reading to prepare for the next block. But before she opens the book, her eyes happen to glance over to her bookcase.

They notice the green cover of her old copy of *Curative Education*. She bought that book many years ago, during her training, but she has never really opened it, although she always meant to. She finds herself putting down the book she intended to read and pulling *Curative Education* off the shelf. "What the heck," she thinks to herself, "might as well see what Steiner has to say about all this."

The very first sentence hits her hard. "We have, as you know, quite a number of children whose development has been arrested and whom we have now to educate—or again, *to heal*, in so far as this is possible."

"Yes!" thinks the teacher, "That's it exactly!" From her very first days in teacher training she had felt the responsibility implicit in Waldorf Education to be a healing education. It used to be so much clearer how to work in a healing way with the children. Looking at the temperaments, working with the stories from the curriculum, working with rhythm and movement in the morning circle and everything else she learned in her teacher training used to be enough to create significant amounts of healing and change in the children. Now there were more and more for whom all of that didn't seem to be enough, and the tools she was being handed were at best accommodations, but this is what was missing. The healing was missing. Every suggestion she had ever been given amounted more or less to a band-aid, something to make the child more manageable perhaps, but no one was talking about healing. For the first time in a long time, the teacher felt some hope. If Steiner used the word heal, maybe that's just what he meant. Maybe more was possible than she had been led to believe.

★

In the second paragraph of *Curative Education*, Steiner gives us a thought that if we allow to work into us becomes a salve for dissolving the fear and feelings of incompetence that many of us have felt so deeply. He says "the very things we notice in incompletely developed children, in children who are suffering from some illness or abnormality, can also be discerned in the so-called normal life of soul; only, they show themselves there less plainly, and in order to recognize them we must be able to practice a more intimate and close observation. In some corner of the life of soul of every human being lurks a quality, or tendency, that would commonly be called abnormal." Just this little thought can begin to give us some hope. The children we have found so mysterious aren't that mysterious at all. Somewhere we are just like them. If we can begin to understand our own "abnormalities" we can begin to understand the children.

In this paragraph from the beginning of the first lecture of *Curative Education,* Steiner offers a key for beginning to learn to breathe.

Suppose we have here the physical body of the human being, as it confronts us while the little child is growing. Then we have the life of soul, rising up as it were—coming forth from this physical body. This life of soul, which can show itself in varied expressions and manifestations, may be normal or it may be abnormal. But now the only possible grounds we can have for speaking of the normality or abnormality of the child's life of soul, or indeed of the life of soul of any human being is that we have in mind something that is normal in the sense of being average. There is no other criterion than the one that is customary among people who abide by ordinary conventions; such people have their ideas of what is to be considered reasonable or clever, and then everything that is *not* an expression of "normal" life of soul (as they understand it) is for them an abnormality. At present there is really no other criterion. That is why the conclusions people come to are so very confused. When they have in this way ascertained the existence of "abnormality," they begin to do—heaven knows what!—believing they are thereby helping to get rid of the abnormality, while all the time they are driving out a fragment of genius! We shall get nowhere at all by applying this kind of criterion, and the first thing the doctor and teacher have to do is reject it and get beyond the stage of making pronouncements as to what is clever or reasonable, in accordance with the habits of thought that prevail today. Particularly in this domain we must refrain from jumping to conclusions, and simply *look at things as they are.* What have we actually before us in the human being?

There is so much in this paragraph. First is the freedom to look away from everything we have been told about "normal" and "abnormal." Every assessment and every evaluation is based on the notion of scale. Someone has arbitrarily created a scale of "normal" and "abnormal" and any child falling outside of the lines of "normal" is given a label that reflects this "abnormality." The words "normal" and "abnormal" create walls that separate us and make real understanding impossible. But Steiner is telling us there is no "normal" or abnormal," and this is why the process of trying to sift out "abnormality" becomes so confused, such a dead end. We assess the child, we give the child a label, we list the things we think the child can't do because of that label, and we leave them to sit in the box we have created for them with no possibility of the notion of real healing available. Steiner makes this an even stronger statement by saying that by doing this we are destroying the genius of the child. This is what is so painful to us as teachers and parents. We have been taught that it is our responsibility to see that genius. This is what the teacher is looking for each morning as she shakes each child's hand. This is the image we carry into our sleep life as a meditation. And then we take the children who need us the most, and send them off to do something that destroys the reality of the very image that gives us the hope and courage to move forward.

What does Steiner mean by doing "heaven knows what"? In Waldorf classrooms all over you can see children sitting on one-legged stools, or children wearing weighted vests or special implements on their hands to help them to write better, or headphones meant to block out extra noise. All of these things are examples of "heaven knows what." If you listen to what the children who have to experience them are saying you will hear them calling themselves names that are very derogatory. They know that these things are not really helping, but they do make them separate from their classmates. They may temporarily and superficially make things easier for a teacher, but they are not helping the child to heal. Steiner has more to say about the reasons these things don't work, but for now it's enough to know that these are some of the things he was referring to when he talks about "destroying the genius."

What a relief to read that Steiner's advice is to reject these evaluations and assessments, no matter how benign they may seem and "get beyond the stage of making pronouncements as to what is clever and reasonable." Another word for this is judgment. We need to get beyond judgments. This is the kind of Ahrimanic influence Steiner talks about in reference to breathing that causes breathing to harden into consuming. So what does Steiner tell us to do? He tells us to learn to *"look at things as they are."* In other words, to replace judgment with observation: "What have we before us in the human being?"

Many of us think we know how to observe, but it can be a surprise to discover just how much judgment leaks into our observations. Here is a simple exercise. Think of a stone, or find one to observe. Think of four or five adjectives to describe that stone. It's not difficult to come up with five adjectives that are not judgments when we are looking at a stone. Words like black, white, speckled, rough, smooth or sharp, come to mind fairly easily. Only the most fanciful resort to judgments about stones such as "it is listening to the earth" or "it is speaking about its love for the gnomes." An observation means only that which you can observe with your normal day-to-day senses. Perhaps if someone was clairvoyant they could perceive a stone speaking to gnomes, but most of us can't do that yet. Anything that is not an observation is a judgment. If may be poetical, but it doesn't belong to this first step Steiner is giving us toward learning to heal children.

When we move up to the plant kingdom it's still fairly easy to merely observe. The plant can be green, have red veins running through the leaves, it's leaves might be thick or thin, have sharp points or be rounded. It may have a flower that is red, pink, orange, yellow, etc. But we could not say that the plant "dances in the wind." We might observe that the plant is moved by the wind, but we cannot observe anything indigenous to the plant itself that allows it to move out of its own resources. We can't really even say that the plant is growing. We might know that it does. We may have measured it from the time it was a seedling. But growing happens too slowly for us to see it in the moment, and we can only speculate as to whether or not the plant will continue to grow.

When we move again to the animal kingdom, things get a little more difficult. We can say that an animal has four legs, or white fur. It may have whiskers or pointy ears. Its fur may be curly, soft, or rough. It may be scaly or have feathers. But we cannot say that the animal is friendly, nice, obstinate, or happy without resorting to judgments. This is the interesting thing about judgments. A judgment may be positive or it may be negative, but in learning to *just observe* we have to be willing to let go of all kinds of judgments. This becomes more difficult when we are looking at animals, but it becomes really hard when we are looking at humans.

We can observe that a person has blue eyes. We can say that their hands are small in proportion to their limbs. They can have black, brown, blond, or red hair. Their hair may be straight or curly or wavy. They may have freckles. Their ears may lay flat on their head or not. All of these kinds of things we can observe. But we cannot observe that they are cheerful, morose, naughty, or helpful without resorting to judgment.

The importance of knowing the difference has to do with something Steiner talks about in *The Foundations of Human Experience.** It has to do with the importance of sympathy and antipathy and their relationship to love. Steiner tells us that love is the balance between sympathy and antipathy. The ability to observe without judgment is related to our ability to love. Judgment impedes our ability to love, because it is always something created arbitrarily out of our own opinions. We make positive judgments out of sympathy. We make negative judgments out of antipathy. Both of these are reflections of our own self-projections. Love requires equanimity. It requires soul balance, and this is something we can build up when we teach ourselves to observe without judgment. When we can do this we create a quiet, still space within ourselves where something very important is possible. Balance creates a still place within us where things can begin to be heard.

When we are working with a child, this calm, quiet place of balance is what makes it possible for us to begin to perceive the genius of the child. This is the image of the child's higher self. The image we then carry with us through meditation into our sleep life. This is the image we offer up to the child's angel so that the angel

---

* Rudolf Steiner, *The Foundations of Human Experience* (Anthroposophic Press, 1996). These 14 lectures are the core of the training given by Rudolf Steiner to the teachers of the first Waldorf School. Also available as *Study of Man*.

can begin to work with us to heal the child. It is the child's angel that can then whisper something new the next morning, some idea of how we can begin to work with the child differently. Learning to observe without judgment is learning to breathe. It is learning to connect what is *without* with what is *within*. It creates a subtle cord between the child and the teacher, where understanding can begin to flow between the two. This is where we begin the work of healing. We know that the difficulties the child experiences are identical to difficulties we have had ourselves. This is what will lead us to the next step.

2. WARMING

On Monday morning the teacher awoke feeling more hopeful than she had in a long time. Nothing had changed, but something had begun to shift. In just those first few paragraphs Steiner had given the teacher a reason to put aside all the things that hadn't been working. Finding a label was not the answer; nor was doing "God knows what"—like bringing special paraphernalia into the classroom—the answer; and the answer was not the making of a list of things the child seemed unable to do. She didn't know what the answer was yet, but at least she had been given something to do. She could observe. Just observe. She didn't know why exactly or what she would get from doing it, but it was something she could begin to work with. Steiner spoke of healing in the very first sentence of the first lecture of the book. If he said that, then he must have had an idea of how a teacher was supposed to get there.

That morning in the classroom things looked pretty much the same. Nothing was miraculously changed overnight. But instead of noting all the things that were going wrong and feeling despair about them, the teacher tried as hard as she could to just observe. She found that she could not think of how frustrated she was by the children's behavior and simply observe them at the same time, and so she felt less frustrated. While she was observing it was impossible to feel anything but balanced and neutral. She tried to put all the thoughts and words from all those reports out of her mind, and she tried to get a real hold on herself to not feel the fear that went with those words. She just tried to observe. Jasper had dark brown curly hair. He had blue eyes. His skin was pale. Allen had black hair; so black it had blue highlights in it. His eyes were large and golden brown. Max had curly red hair and freckles. His hands and feet were small in comparison to his arms and legs. Alice had strawberry blond hair and blue eyes. She was shorter than many of the children in her class. Sienna was taller than most, and thin. She had light brown hair and grey eyes. Peter was more rounded. His hair was dark blond, straight and fine. His eyes were hazel.

Every day she tried to observe something new. Who had a mole? Who had ears flat to their heads and who had ears that stuck out? What was the shape of their fingernails? How were their limbs proportionate to their bodies? The teacher began to notice something. The more she just observed, the less she was able to think thoughts that were judgments. Steiner says that everything we think affects the children, right down to their organs. The teacher had always felt that the children knew, on some level, what all the adults around them thought about them. The fewer her judgmental thoughts, the more the children began to relax. She realized that all those judgments came out of her feelings; they were led by her emotions. They were astral, and they did not give her ego much room to step in and find a place of equanimity. Fear is just a prayer for what we don't want. By holding these pictures in her mind she had been feeding her fear, and the children had been doing their best to make sure her prayer was answered. Which came first, the thought that Peter might be "developmentally delayed" and therefore couldn't be expected to do any work independently? or was Peter truly incapable of working on his own? This was true for all of the labels the teacher had been handed about her children.

> Let us say the child wants to walk, has the *will* to walk, but cannot. This can become a pathological condition, can become quite conspicuous; it may even happen that at last the child comes to be described as "incapable of learning to walk."[…] So long as the teacher meets the situation with any kind of bias, so long as it can arouse in him or her irritation or excitement—so long will he or she remain incapable of making any progress with the child. Not until the point has been reached where such a phenomenon becomes an objective picture and can be taken with a certain calm and composure as an objective picture for which nothing but compassion is felt—not until then is the necessary mood of soul present in the astral body of the teacher. Once this has come about, the teacher is there by the side of the child in a true relation and will do all else that is needful more or less correctly. (*Curative Education*, Lecture Two)

When we start with just what we can observe we eliminate the negative astrality that comes out of judgment. It is impossible to make a judgment that doesn't have some element of our own emotions involved. Balance is a quiet place within us. When we are working out of this place of balance it's impossible for any little fingers of our astrality to poke their way into the picture. This kind of astrality is always connected to sympathy or antipathy. It has to do with the irritation or excitement Steiner was talking about. When the teacher created balance inside herself something was able to make it's appearance within that quiet, still place in the teacher. The higher self of the child was able to show itself again. This is the "fragment of genius" that Steiner speaks of. It's not that the teacher had forgotten that each child in her care had a higher self, but the fear and confusion of the labels with which she had been presented had gotten in the way of her perceptions. If it is true that our thoughts about the child can create incapacities in the child; if when we think the child can't play without hitting other children; or can't read; or remember things; or do math; or engage creatively in her play, we actually bring about those conditions, then it is also true that when we create within ourselves the ability to see the genius in the child, when we then hold on to that picture tenaciously, we are helping to create those positive things in the child.

This is perhaps one of the most healing things we can do. Learning to just observe allowed for this place of balance and neutrality to open up again, and the pictures of the children's higher selves had a place to live in her. She began to feel hopeful. This allowed her to begin to breathe.

Once she began to really live with the pictures of the higher self she could see again what a good heart Jasper had. She remembered Max's intelligence and real interest in the world. She saw in Sienna the person who truly cared for others and could have empathy. Allen had such a capacity for steadiness and order; and Alice had a genuine feeling for calmness and serenity. In Peter she saw the boy who wanted to come forward, the one who wanted to learn and take part in the world. Each of these children felt the shift in their teacher. Each of them felt how she was trying to reach them. Steiner says we have no idea of the unimportance of all that a teacher says or does not say—of far greater importance is *what* the teacher truly is as a person. The children could feel that the teacher had the desire to become a person who could really help them. They could feel this shift, and they began to have some hope that things might change for the better, that someone might begin to help them. This allowed them to begin to breathe.

The next time the teacher had a parent teacher conference she tried something new. The parents of Jasper, Max, Allen, Alice, Sienna and Peter had become very used to hearing all that was not working. They were defensive before they even entered the room. Parents want their children to be seen. The teacher made a point not to begin the conference with a list of problems. Instead she asked each parent to just describe his or her child. They worked together to just make a physical description of the child. She explained about observation and judgment and they tried to just stick to the facts. Then they made lists of all the things about the child that constituted their higher self. These are the same images every good Waldorf teacher brings into his or her sleep life through meditation each evening. The rest of the conference worked around ways they could support more of these positive things becoming more evident at home and at school. Each parent took a good deep breath. The first in a long time.

The teacher had made a good first step. She thought again about Steiner's words about the importance of who or what the teacher is as a person. Now she had to take a look at herself.

*

In Lecture Two of *Curative Education,* Steiner speaks of the Pedagogical Law. He gives it as a tool to help us influence the four bodies of the child. It looks simple at first. It is not. He says "Any one member of the human being is influenced by the *next highest member,* and only under such influence can that member develop satisfactorily. Thus, whatever is to be effective for the development of the physical body must be living in the etheric body—in *an* etheric body. Whatever is to be effective for the development of an etheric body must be living in an astral body. Whatever is to be effective for the development of an astral body must be living in an ego; and an ego can be influenced only by what is living in a spirit self." He goes on to clarify, "What does this mean in practice? If you find that the etheric body of a child is in some way weakened or deficient, you must form, you must modify, your own astral body in such a way that it can work on the etheric body of the child, correcting and amending it." Then he gives this diagram:

Child		Teacher
Physical Body	:	Etheric Body
Etheric Body	:	Astral Body
Astral Body	:	I (or Ego)
I (or Ego)	:	Spirit Self

Steiner uses the word teacher in the diagram, but this law applies to anyone in the child's life, parents as well as teachers. At first, it seems like another way to add on more guilt, more reasons why we are at fault for the child's difficulties. What is clear is that we have to see ourselves as literally a container for the children. The first step towards making this Pedagogical Law into a useful tool is to take inventory of our own container. How are we? What is the condition of our physical body? Etheric body? Astral body? Our "I"? And what about the Spirit Self? Do we even have a Spirit Self yet? We have to look at ourselves in these five aspects and include in the pictures the state of our four lower senses.*

We start by looking at our physical body. Obviously we have to start by looking at the health of our physical body, but beyond that, what do we need to know? The organ that contains our physical body is our skin. This is the organ for the first of our lower senses; our sense of touch. By this Steiner doesn't mean tactile differentiation; he means: Do we know where our skin is? Are we aware of it as our boundary, the place where we end and where the world begins? Everything to do with how we approach the world starts with the awareness of our own skin. The importance of our skin as

---

* The subject of the twelve senses and their division into three sets of four forms an important part of the basic understanding of the human being through Anthroposophy, and thus Waldorf Education. The four lower or "basal" senses are the senses of touch, life, (self) movement, and balance. See Steiner, *The Foundations of Human Experience*, Lecture Eight.

a boundary will have very much to do with understanding the conditions of the Curative Polarities later on, but for now it's enough to begin to take inventory of our own awareness. Do I live too deeply within my own skin? or am I trapped outside of my body? Both ends of this spectrum results in a feeling of disconnect with one's own skin. The first can cause us to approach the world too strongly. Others may find us abrasive. They may feel we take up too much space when we enter a room. People experience us as pushy. Or the opposite can be true. If we are stuck too far outside of our skin the world approaches us too closely. We are too aware of the world and so it causes us pain. This means others can experience us as being overly sensitive. We can seem very self-involved. What is our tolerance for contact? How do we approach the world?

Then we have to look at our etheric body. How strong and healthy is your life body? This has to do with our sense of life. Do you know when you are hungry, cold, tired, and sick? Do you know when you feel well? Both our etheric body and our sense of life thrive on rhythm. Do you have a rhythm? Do you know when you need to get up each morning in order to have time enough to feel prepared to meet the day, or do you stagger out of bed at the last possible minute and then play catch-up all day. Do you know when you need to go to bed in order to feel ready for the next day? If you do know these things, do you do them? Are you as committed to obeying your own care and feeding instructions as you would like the parents in your class to be about seeing to the care and feeding instructions of the children you work with? Do you know what you need to eat to best serve your body? Long term, is the caffeine really worth it? Or the alcohol? There are many diets popular now that have an excarnating effect. These can be addicting, because they make us feel a bit euphoric for a while, but in the end they take away from our ability to be grounded and present. We need to care for ourselves so that we are better able to serve others, but simultaneously we have to avoid the danger of becoming self-absorbed by our own health.

The best gauge of the health of a teacher's etheric body is their classroom management. One of the meditations Steiner gives in *Curative Education* is the point and periphery meditation. He says to imagine a point within a circle. And then imagine a circle containing a point. This exercise is a tool for making our minds more flexible, and an opportunity to practice what he calls etheric thinking. This will be discussed more later on, but for now take it as a way to understand how you need to use your etheric body (and your ego or I) to hold your class. The teacher is the point. The children are the periphery. As a teacher, you stand with your ego as the "point" in the classroom, and the children figuratively form the circle, but you have to be able to reach out from the point of your ego to the periphery of the room using your etheric body. You have to hold the entire class with this etheric body. This means it has to be strong enough and large enough and elastic enough to reach to the farthest corner of the room. It has to be aware of everything that is going on in the room, and hold the possibility for wholeness. Teachers who resort to uncontrolled yelling at their classes are not able to hold them etherically, and so the astral dives in and tempers are lost.

Next we look at the astral body. Steiner tells us we can observe the condition of the soul forces when we observe a person walking. Observe yourself. Is there anything your walk tells you about yourself? How do you step on the earth? Are you able to move in sync and in balance? The astral body can claim the world of the animals, which live in pure emotion, and the world of the angels, who have transformed their emotions into something that they use to serve humanity. Is your astral body more at home in the world of the animals or the world of angels? Are you riding your horse, or is your horse riding you? When we look at ourselves physically we have to take our physical balance into account, but our physical balance is a mirror of our emotional balance and spiritual balance. So are we aware of when we are in emotional and spiritual balance? Can we feel when we tilt off of center and do we know what to do about it? Going back to the things that support our sense of life can be helpful in gaining insight into our state of balance. It's hard to be in emotional and spiritual balance when we are too tired, or too hungry or sick and not even aware of it. Beyond this though, have we looked at our own biography and identified the things that would cause us to be out of balance? Have we worked through those things? None of us gets through life without some kind of trauma or sorrow. When we work them through they become tools. When we have not worked them through they become excuses. If we are still using our past as an excuse not to do our work in the present, willing to let others pick up the slack, then we have work to do in our astral body.

Are you aware of when you working out of your I or ego? Can you feel the times you stand before your class and are truly present with them, feeling solidly grounded in your feet? Are you aware of how your class reacts to the strength of your ego? Do they feel too much sympathy or antipathy from you, or do they feel the balance between the two, which Steiner calls real love? Steiner says that humor is the first and most essential qualification for a teacher. Do you have a sense of humor? Not in a way that adds astrality to the classroom, but one that comes out of real human warmth, the humor of life. Steiner says that true humor is a sign of true spirituality. He also says "You may have mastered every possible clever method and device but you will not be able to educate these children unless you have the necessary humor."

We can become aware of our ego when we look back at our life. A portion of our sense of movement has to do with our ability to form an intention and follow it through. We see this when we look back at our life and see the pattern. We see that our sense of movement has led us to do all the things that were necessary in order to be at the right place at the current moment. We feel our life has made sense, even if it has been hard, or we wish certain things had gone differently. If you feel a sense of gratitude for where your life has taken you, you can thank your ego working appropriately with your sense of your own movement, the part of you that was able to discriminate right or wrong choices and helped you to stay on track.

Then we come to the tricky part. In order to help the children formulate their ego in the right way we have to be working out of our Spirit Self. We don't have a Spirit Self. Yet. This is a conundrum. In *Curative Education*, Steiner advises meditating on the Spirit Self. This is like a prayer to those spiritual beings who are the same ones that live behind the Genius of Language. As we begin to have a feeling for what lives in language, what lives in speech, we begin to understand these beings. Steiner says that if we want to work with children we will be brought in contact with these beings. We have to appeal to them, because they are more highly developed than we are. They have a Spirit Self and we need their help if our work is to have life.

Another thing to keep in mind is that every time we attempt to use our ego to guide and transform our astral body we are building up the potential for our future Spirit Self. Steiner says that eventually, as part of our evolution, our ego will transform and take charge of first our astral, then our etheric, and finally our physical bodies. Now the higher beings have to do that work for us, but some day they will be under our own jurisdiction. If we want to work in a healing way with the children we have to start now by working out of our ego to transform our lower astrality.

Another resource that Steiner recommends in *Curative Education* is the book *How to Know Higher Worlds.* There, too, Steiner tells us to pay attention to our bodily and spiritual health. All of the things he recommends there for someone interested in obtaining insights into the spiritual world are relevant to obtaining insights on the way to becoming better curative teachers and parents.

At this point we are faced with a choice. We can look at the Pedagogical Law and it can be the catalyst for an enormous amount of guilt. We can feel so badly for all our shortcomings that we become immobilized. We can read about this and feel that since we obviously will never obtain perfection in this we may as well not start. This would not be the right approach. We stand before the children and we expect them to heal. We expect them to take up their work and to do their best. They expect the same of us. We do not expect the children to be perfect. And they do not expect us to be perfect; nor do they need us to be. But if we are going to stand in front of them as honest human beings, we have to be striving. Remember, it is not what we say or do, but what we are that will make us healing educators. What we are trying to become is the best reflection of who we are. So we don't need to choose to feel guilty. There is another option.

After breathing, the next of the life processes is warming. Karl

König describes this poetically as "finding a shelter in which to become established." We begin our relationship with the world through breathing, but

> The breathing must become localized; a "house" must be built that is very tender yet very strong, and this 'house' can only be built if the warmth outside is different from the warmth inside, so that the warmth builds something into which the air can enter and leave again. It is as if, with the breathing process, we start to weave a kind of fabric, and the warming process constructs the loom around the warp. (*A Living Physiology*, p. 67)

The breathing process is brought into a kind of form. It is warmed through and thereby starts to form itself. The process of warming is connected to our sense of warmth. This means it has to do with the regulation of things, including our emotions. Anger is very connected to our sense of warmth, but ideally the kind of anger that is a catalyst for change. If we can't feel anger in the right way we can't feel love. The sense of warmth lives in the bloodstream, the same stream that carries our ego through our limbs and metabolic system. In the limbs and metabolic system the ego lives at the periphery, but in the head the ego is the central body. It lives in the two-petaled lotus of discretion, which is our third eye. This is where we have to build our house. It is a house of warmth, and of real love, the kind that comes from our ego. The process of warming is connected to the sun; emulating the warming love of the sun. So warming is a kind of building up of a place within us of warming love. We could call this compassion. The danger in warming is that it can become a fever, it can become burning. If we don't check our warmth within the boundaries of the house within us it can become a force for destruction.

In the first lecture of *Curative Education* Steiner makes these two points about teaching:

> If the teacher can feel his way right into the situation, if he is able himself to feel the stoppage that the child feels, and able at the same time out of his own energy to evoke in his soul a deep compassion with the child's experience, then he will develop in his own astral body an understanding for

> the situation the child is in and will gradually succeed in eliminating in himself all subjective reaction of feeling when faced with this phenomenon in the child. By ridding himself of every trace of subjective reaction of feeling the teacher educates his own astral body.

and:

> So long as the teacher meets the situation with any kind of bias, so long as it can arouse in him irritation or excitement—so long will he remain incapable of making any real progress with the child. Not until the point has been reached where such a phenomenon becomes an objective picture for which nothing but compassion is felt-not until then is the necessary mood of soul present in the astral body of the teacher. Once this has come about, the teacher is there by the side of the child in a true relation and will do all else that is needful more or less rightly.

Here we come to the second option: Another way of looking at the Pedagogical Law, not as yet another bludgeon, but as a tool to access our compassion. The Pedagogical Law asks us to take a look at ourselves. We take inventory to see all the places we have work to do. The places where we are stuck. Obviously we look at these things in order to make improvements, but here we have something indigenous to anthroposophy; we are asked to make improvements on ourselves, but not for our own glorification. There are plenty of options today to help us toward self-improvement. The difference here is that we are asked to get better not for our own sakes, but for the sake of the others we might be able to serve, just as we take up an inner life not for our own spiritual advancement, but so that we are better able to help others advance.

The by-product of this kind of self-awareness is compassion. We look inside ourselves and see where we are stuck. We are asked to live into the experience of the child and approach with empathy and compassion the places where the child is stuck. This is the real gift of the Pedagogical Law. Taken up in the right way, it becomes a tool for breaking down the barriers between the child and the teacher. The children can no longer be looked at as having disabilities that make them separate from us, as having conditions beyond our comprehension. The places where the children are stuck are mirrored inside of each of us in the places where we are stuck, and as we learn to heal ourselves we learn to know firsthand the things that will heal the children. Instead of being fodder for guilt, our wounds and shortcomings become our treasures. They constitute our toolbox of templates for understanding everything the children present to us. We have been taught that the things that have hurt us the most are the things we must work the hardest to conceal. We have been taught to feel shame. We think we are the only ones who have experienced death, depression, rape, catastrophic illness, and true traumas. We are taught that children who have experienced these things are "damaged" and may never develop beyond these things in a healthy way. This is untrue. All of us have a tale of sorrow to tell, and all of us have reacted to our sorrows in various ways. When we begin to work with the Pedagogical Law in the right way these things can no longer separate us; they become the threads of compassion that connect us. This is what "warming" can look like. By taking a look at all the places in us that have caused us discomfort, sorrow, or pain, we begin to build a little workshop in our hearts; a place where the difficulties of the children can be taken in and lived into. When we begin to do this, when we begin to live into the child's experience in the right way, we will begin to know what to do.

*

The teacher began with some light housekeeping. She started off by trying to alter the habits that she knew were not going to serve her in the long term. She needed a schedule. It was easy to make one, but difficult to see it through. It takes three weeks to change a habit and the teacher had some habits to change. She had to decide what time each day she could commit to coming home. This is a balancing act. When you are working collectively, as is attempted in a Waldorf school, it doesn't really work to say, "I need to leave at three every day," if that means that one's colleagues have to pick up the slack, but finding a balance is possible. What time can we commit to heading for home and still take up the committee work and faculty meetings that we need to do in order to carry our load in the school? One thing to look at is what do we do after the meetings. Do we linger with one or two colleagues and rehash the meeting? Do we find something to do in our classroom that is going to take us much longer to complete because it's the end of the day and we're exhausted? These were the sorts of things the teacher needed to look at, and then once she had found an appropriate time for her workday to be over she needed to make sure she honored that. She made a plan that would guarantee she was home every evening in time for dinner with her family and in time to help put her children to bed. Then she had to look at what time she put herself to bed, and, again, she had to make a commitment to herself to be in bed every night at her appointed bedtime, and then get up at the same time everyday, with enough time to start her day prepared. The three cups of coffee had to go. She had to give serious consideration to having breakfast. In Waldorf Teacher Training we hear that "rhythm replaces strength." It does. All of these things seemed superficial, but in the end they were very important. A side benefit was that the next time she included the importance of rhythm in her parent evening agenda she did not feel like a liar.

As she began to look at herself, the teacher also began to look at the children differently.

When she thought about Jasper being so frustrated that he knocked his desk over, it wasn't hard to imagine her own frustration when, trying as hard as she could to do something, it just would not work. She remembered the look in his eyes just before he dumped his desk, the look that was soft and vulnerable and seemed to ask for someone to help him. This was exactly how she was feeling that day. The work of understanding the children had seemed too hard, and she just wanted someone to help her. She didn't dump her desk over, but she knew that sometimes she felt frustrated enough to imagine throwing something.

She thought about the time she had been in the hospital recovering from surgery and how much it hurt her if someone just jostled the bed. She could see in Sienna's gestures of protection that same kind of sensitivity to having anything come too close.

When she remembered how she sometimes wakes in the middle of the night only to begin replaying in her mind the vile deeds of a colleague, deeds that happened years ago, that she can't seem to let it go of, it's not hard to understand how Allen can perseverate with the cat story.

Coming into middle age, and the forgetfulness that comes with it, was a clue to understanding Alice and thinking back to the first times she tried to navigate a computer; how she compared herself to the ones, younger than herself, who were patiently trying to help her, and who already understood the machine so fluently while she struggled just to find words to ask the right questions. This was also a lead into why Peter often chose to check out when the pace of the classroom moved past him quicker than he could link in.

*

All of these experiences are part of what is meant by "living into" the experience of the child. The next part is to truly let the experience live; to let it take root and even sleep in the place of "warming," the little shelter we build inside ourselves for understanding. When we "live into" something in the right way we don't push for conclusions too soon. We have to let the things sink into us to a place where they can be understood with our hearts, not our intellect. Our heart has to do the thinking, and it is the angel of the child who will speak to our angel about the things we might do when we have the understanding. If we push with our intellect and try to connect the dots too quickly we will fall right back into the danger of making judgments, the thing we are trying to avoid. This is how we avoid becoming fanatics. In the second lecture, Steiner says:

> This will mean that while we must do our best to come to an understanding of such illnesses, we cannot expect to be able at once in each single case to use methods and treatment that accord with the picture we have in our understanding. It is, on this account, very important that there shall be no fanatics among you. It will not do for you to set out on this work of Curative Education in a fanatical spirit, not knowing how to judge the scope and bearing of some truth, when it is a question of applying esoteric knowledge in practical life.

This is why we just let the understanding that compassion can give us sit gently in our hearts and wait until something wiser than ourselves is ready to give us an answer as to what the next step should look like.

If we do not do this, if we allow ourselves to be catapulted out of this calm place of understanding into some fiery desire to act immediately, we will find ourselves in the place of fever that Steiner is talking about as the danger of "warming" going out of control. We become destructive. We will face the possibility of burning up. We will become so enamored of our own astral speculations that we will become fanatical.

*

For now, the teacher was wise enough to just sit with the new understandings. She could feel that something within her was truly warmed. She still didn't know what she was going to do, but she knew that she was in a much better place to begin than she had been before. She could breathe through her perceptions of the children and bring those perceptions into the shelter of compassion within her. Now she was ready for the "nourishing."

3. NOURISHING

In Waldorf education the concept of the four "temperaments" is used as a tool for understanding children.* The temperaments have to do with a preponderance of one or another of the four bodies working into a person in ways that affect that person's personality. A preponderance of the forces of the physical body results in a melancholic temperament, while the etheric body's prevalence results in a phlegmatic temperament; when the astral body is most ascendant, a sanguine temperament results, while a preponderance of ego forces results in a choleric temperament. Each temperament comes with its own gifts and peccadilloes. We work as parents and teachers to try to balance the temperament, and there are certain tools for doing this. For example, as adults, we can consciously work on ourselves, cultivating and balancing elements of the temperaments in our own soul life, which has a balancing influence on the children in our care.

For the most part, working with the temperaments is an excellent tool, but more and more there is a portion in each class of children for whom the pictures of the temperaments are, to begin with, no longer relevant. When the right kind of healing can take place for them, the temperaments can again become useful, but we often have to start with other tools. These are the pictures of the *curative polarities*. For these children, one of the biggest difficulties occurs when we try to understand their condition through the lens of the temperaments when this lens no longer applies. When children have moved into the pictures of the curative polarities, attempting to understand them through the temperaments will only foster misunderstanding. They will of course sense that they are misunderstood, and they will resent it, as well they should.

---

*   See Rudolf Steiner: "The Four Temperaments" in *Anthroposophy in Everyday Life* (Anthroposophic Press, 1995); and *Discussions with Teachers*, pp. 36 ff. (Anthroposophic Press, 1997).

When working with the temperaments, we aim toward balance or a "rounding out," but we are not looking at conditions which can debilitate, conditions that prevent the child from becoming their truest selves. When the child has moved into the realm of curative education there will be areas in need of significant change or healing; areas that are blocked in ways that prevent the child from becoming their truest, highest self. When we look into the pictures of the polarities, these pictures will resonate to some degree in all of us. All of us have areas that fit these pictures, but for many of us those things are not preventing us from achieving what we are capable of doing. It is a matter of degree.

If we think back to the children we met in the first chapter, it would be simple to think of Jasper as a choleric, of Max as a sanguine, of Alice as a phlegmatic, and of Sienna as a melancholic. We might think this way, and we might try to work with them out of this understanding, but we would only frustrate them and ourselves. We would have the feeling that everything we knew was not working. To truly understand the conditions of these children, and to begin to be able to live into these conditions in the way Steiner describes in lectures three, four, and five of *Curative Education* is the precursor to being able to heal.

When we begin to work with the polarities, we first have to understand that we are not dealing with a preponderance of one body, but instead looking at the way the four bodies should unite and work together. Steiner describes the ideal working together of the four bodies as a lemniscate. If we look at the area of our head we should be able to experience that our ego is the central innermost body. The astral body surrounds the ego, which is surrounded by the etheric body. In our head, the physical body is the outermost component. Knock on your skull and you will experience this. In the metabolic-limb system the lemniscate reverses itself. There the physical body is innermost. Think of the bones of your skeleton. This is surrounded by the etheric and then astral bodies. In our limbs and metabolic system the ego is the outermost component. If you were to stand up, in balance, heel-to-toe, with your arms straight out to the sides and your head up, and then close your eyes, you may begin to experience this. If you pay attention long enough you will notice that in your head you can sense the place of inner rest. You should be able to feel the place behind your third eye where you have inner stillness. This is true balance, the real balance of the vestibular system. Simultaneously, you can perhaps experience a warming or a feeling of awareness surrounding your limbs. This is an experience of the ego that should be present in our skin as it moves through our metabolic-limb system through the warmth of our blood. Ideally, this lemniscate should live in each of us. But there are times when it doesn't. There are situations where the four bodies do not come together in this way, and when they don't we then have the conditions known as the curative polarities.

The first two conditions have to do with the process of waking up in the morning. Every night, when we fall asleep, our astral and ego bodies journey out from our physical and etheric bodies and live for a while in the vastness of the cosmos. In the morning, when we wake up, the astral and ego bodies need to return to their earthly home, which is our etheric and physical bodies. "Waking up" should be an awareness of the integrity of my own self, contained within my own skin. We should be both aware of ourselves and of the world surrounding us. Through our ego, we should be able to experience the force of the earth we call gravity. The ego, as it enters into the physical body, enables the physical body to overcome gravity, so that we can stand upright. The ego actually makes the physical body light, so that it can overcome the weight of gravity. Steiner tells us that when we are able to walk in the right way we are actually placing ourselves with our ego organization right into the actual gravity of the earth. We enter into a direct connection with the earthly.

Through our etheric body we are able to enter the force of buoyancy. When our ego can work with our etheric body correctly then our ego can experience and live within the force of buoyancy.

When the ego is able to work correctly with the astral body it can experience the force of "light." Steiner points out that the traditional meaning of "light" is not what is meant here, but "light" in the sense of an illuminating force: a kind of etheric force that enables our senses to illuminate the world for us. There is a kind of illuminating etheric "light" that enables us to perceive not only through our eyes, but also through what we hear, smell, taste and touch. When our astral body is able to work correctly it makes a direct connection with this "light." Near the beginning of lecture three of *Curative Education,* Steiner says "when we wake up, we not only come into connection with the light that is within us, but, turning aside as it were from the light that is within us, we member ourselves into the light that streams through the external world." He says we also "member," (German: "*gliedern*"; integrate or organize) ourselves into the chemical forces at work in the world around us.

All this is what normally entails "waking up." It should always happen, but it doesn't; and when it doesn't the first two of the six polarities are manifested. What should happen is that, as we wake up, our astral and ego bodies are breathed into our physical and etheric bodies. They are breathed in, and then they must breathe out until they reach the point of balance. This is our skin. Waking should be an experience of our skin, a daily renewal or confirmation that says: "here I am; I am this being living within this container." But it does happen that the astral and ego bodies are breathed in, and, instead of breathing out, they get stuck. Steiner says they may get stuck in a particular organ, for example the liver.

We don't need to ponder this too deeply at this point. The important thing is to live into this picture; the astral and ego are present within the physical and etheric, but they are stuck too deeply within us. They are stuck, but they want to come to the place of balance. They want to be able to make contact with our container, our skin, so that we can truly wake up and begin to take in the world. What do we do when something is stuck? If we are trying to get through a door, and we find it is stuck we give it a good push. This is the gesture of the first condition Steiner talks about. When this push occurs in the physical body the result is an epileptic seizure. Epilepsy is really an attempt of the whole organism, all four bodies, to come to their proper alignment. The astral and ego "push" to try to come to contact with the skin, which should be their proper home, and the result is a seizure. This is why Steiner refers to the first polarity as "Epileptic." We don't use this word in practical working because we would be confusing ourselves. Karl

König referred to this condition as "overly irritable." Another way to refer to this condition very simply is to say "thick-skinned."

An epileptic event in the physical body is a seizure, but we can also have "seizures" in our astral body or ego. When we are working with a child who has seemingly inexplicable outbursts of anger or aggression we may be looking at a kind of "astral" seizure. When a child is in this "thick-skinned" condition we may experience them as poking and pushing. Because their awareness is stuck too far inside themselves, they need to poke and push on everything around them in order to know where they are. When we are aware of our skin, and even (etherically) a little beyond it, we don't need to bump into something in order to know that it is there. When we haven't achieved this awareness we have to hit something first. This is a device of *location* and the thing we are trying to locate is ourselves. Think back to Jasper, and how as he entered the classroom he caused so much consternation because he crashed, hit, bumped, pushed, and stepped on everything and everyone. Jasper was not doing this because he took an innate pleasure in destruction. He was doing it because the only way he knew how to know where he existed was to crash, hit, bump, push, and stomp.

When a child is in a "thick-skinned" condition he or she never fully attains consciousness. They are not able to fully wake up and connect with their ego into the forces of gravity, buoyancy, light, or the chemical forces, because their astral and ego bodies never make it far enough out to connect with their skin, which is the home the ego is seeking in the metabolic-limb system in order to wake up. They also don't make the right connection to the core of balance in the vestibular system. Because of this, they don't make real connections with the outer world. They will seem to lack social and intellectual interest. We may try to force them to take an interest by shaming them into it. We say things like "Why don't you look where you're going?" or "Look what you did! You stepped all over Janey's lunch basket! How do you think Janey feels about that?" We may think that by having these kind of intellectual discussions about what we perceive as the child's insensitivity we are bringing them to a place of being sensitive. We are not. Until we begin to understand why the child is acting this way we will get nowhere.

The child is not making an intellectual decision to be destructive. They are just trying to find themselves in space. This does not mean they shouldn't be brought to a different awareness; ultimately they are responsible for their actions, but until we have addressed the root cause we will not get very far.

When you are trying to teach this child you may notice that they are one of the students who know everything before you explain it or talk about it. They will not wait for instructions before they begin. They jump into things head first, but then suddenly they are drowning. They have no idea what to do. They may begin to cry. When you are teaching them to read they will try to guess the word before they look at it or try to sound it out. They may read the ending sounds first, because we all know whoever gets to the end first, wins! They will have a difficult time with music, because they are not able to grasp rhythm, or that music is something that should be done in unison. Again, whoever gets to the end of the song first wins, right?

The child in this condition will be very gravity-bound. The ego isn't able to properly work into the physical, and thus the child does not experience the lightness that should allow them to overcome gravity. This is evident in the way they move; how they walk and run and sit in a chair. Because they are not able to overcome gravity they will not be able to come to balance in the right way. This will be observable in their physical balance, but it will also have ramifications in their emotional and spiritual balance as well. This overabundance of gravity will manifest in their work: it will be heavy and dark; when they paint they will not like to blend their colors.

Steiner says we will experience children in this condition as being "giddy." If you have ever experienced a child who is laughing in a raucous, loud, joyless kind of way you have experienced the "giddiness" Steiner is talking about. You see it on the playground when the play goes over the top; when the child begins to "spin out." The activity is no longer play. The child is not in control of his or her actions, and there is no joy for them in this kind of running amok.

Children in this condition may have moral difficulties. Because they are not able to come out of themselves enough to perceive the "other," they will have a hard time equating their actions with the results. Steiner says they may have a tendency to hoard things, which could become kleptomania. This can begin in early childhood with a tendency to hoard sounds. " Ba, Ba, Ba, Ba." They may collect little bits of sounds and repeat them, loudly, for long periods of time.

When a child is in this condition they will not sweat, and you may notice that they have a "dust like" odor to them.

This is a pre-birth condition, which means a condition of contraction. The child in this condition will be contracted, and have a hard time trying to expand. If you think of the fight or flight reaction to fear, they are in the fight end of this spectrum; and they are experiencing fear. This is something we will expand on later.

We can also have the opposite of this condition. The astral/ego enters the physical/etheric body on waking. But this time, instead of getting stuck, it streams out past the skin. This child lives in a disembodied condition. They literally do not live within the boundary of their skin. Steiner calls this the "hysteric" condition. He says this because ,without some kind of healing, the child could be at risk for "hysteria" later in life. Karl König calls this the "overly sensitive" condition. Working with it day-to-day we can call it "thin-skinned."

Here we have too much consciousness of the world, and, because the child is overly consciousness of everything around them, the world causes them pain. They live with constant soul pain because everything seems to come too close to them, to affect them too personally. Their perceptions may not be accurate, but that won't prevent them from reacting as if the things they feel and perceive are true. Because the world causes them so much pain they will have a difficult time making a right relationship to it. Because they live so far out on the periphery they will become overly aware of the thoughts and feelings of others. They will literally read your mind.

Because the world causes them pain they will have a hard time engaging their will to work within the world. As soon as they try to engage in something they experience pain, and so they back away from the activity. This causes their movements to appear restless or jerky. Actions cause them fear. With every new task they have this inner experience: "Oh! I am being asked to create something! I see in my mind how beautiful it will be! I will make this perfect thing! But... it will never be as beautiful as I have imagined it. It will never be as beautiful, and yet I have to make it anyway." Because of this they will have a very hard time beginning their work. They may sit hunched over their work, so that no one can see it. They will have an exaggerated sense of how much others are interested in everything they are doing.

These children have too much levity or buoyancy in them. Their body becomes in a way too light to make the right connection with gravity. You will see this in the gesture of their walking. Their work will be small, light, and tentative. When they paint, their colors will run together too much. Because they have too much levity they will have a hard time coming to physical balance. Soul balance and spiritual balance will also be reflected in this difficulty. They may flip-flop in their emotions.

Children in this condition will have too many secretions of every kind. They may wet themselves or defecate unknowingly. They sweat, and have slime and mucus from every available orifice. They are leaky in their emotions and in their posture as well. They may puddle themselves over their desks with arms spilling over into their neighbor's territory. Steiner tells us we may notice a smell of decay about them.

Sienna is a picture of a child caught in the condition of this polarity. Her overreactions and fear are a picture of "thin-skinnedness."

This condition implies that the child is living in an "after death" condition of expansion. This may be reflected in the etheric rhythm of three and a half days. Often, when they have a meltdown you can trace the catalyst back to an event that happened three and a half days previously. They live in the "flight" end of the fight or flight spectrum. Again we have to be aware of the condition of fear that this implies.

These two conditions are two sides of the same coin. Although when we begin working with a child we may have to start by addressing primarily one manifestation first, we will eventually be confronted with the opposite side of the coin. Remember how Jasper gave his teacher the look of vulnerability just before he threw his chair? This was a moment when thick-skinnedness flipped over to thin-skinnedness, and then rapidly flipped again. Had the teacher known how to react at just that moment, the chair might never have flown. Towards the end of lecture two in *Curative Education,* Steiner gives a clue to help us understand how this flip-flop can occur. He describes a rhythm that can set itself up so that the child's astral/ego first takes hold too deeply, and then flips to become too weak. When we can begin to live into this experience that the child has—this fluctuation between taking hold too deeply and then too weakly—if we can live into this with love, we will see that with time the rhythm is overcome and that the child will begin to do things that are a manifestation of genius. These pictures of "thick-skinned" and "thin-skinned" are not given to us as labels. They are not meant as new boxes we can deposit the children in. They are *conditions,* which can be lived into with love and compassion and the right kind of imagination so that we can understand what stands before us in the child at any given moment. These two polarities are a pendulum. They move. They shift. And they move and shift between four different bodies so that we always have to be asking ourselves, not only which end of the polarity are we dealing with at any given moment of the day, but in which body and how does our approach have to shift accordingly.

The next set of polarities are more static. They do not have to do with how we wake in the morning, but are a more steady condition. If the ego organization locates too strongly in the head, but not enough in the metabolic-limb system, we see a condition Steiner refers to as "sulphur poor." We might also say "iron."

A child with not enough sulphur or too much iron will take in impressions. These impressions should find a home in our metabolic-limb system from which they can be brought back as memories when we need or want to access them, but in the iron child the impressions don't make it down into the metabolic-limb system. The metabolic-limb system is too weak, not enough of the ego organization is able to work there, and so the impressions are constantly pushed back. The ideas cannot be digested, and because they are not digested they keep coming back again and again, long after the first impression was made. These impressions can become fixed ideas. Alan's need to keep repeating the story about the cat is an example of a fixed idea that won't go away, that can't be digested. Because their head is so full of a very limited number of impressions that they can't get rid of, it is very difficult for these children to take in new impressions. They may sit through a whole Main Lesson and be unable at the end to tell you anything about it. This is not because their attention is wandering. They may try very hard to follow you, but there is just no room in their head for a new idea to make its way in.

The iron condition makes the child very jumpy. They may be prone to ticks, or repetitive movements. They may only be comfortable moving in straight lines, and may only perceive the world in straight lines. When they write something in their Main Lesson Book they may go over the same letters again and again. They want to have social interactions with other people, but they don't know how to go about it. Their "conversation" may amount to endless repetitions of ideas or facts that never seem to go away.

The opposite of this condition occurs when there is not enough ego in the head, but too much in the metabolic-limb system. Here there is too much sulphur at work. The ideas are drawn quickly from the head, and sucked into the metabolic-limb system where they stay, as if they had fallen into a swamp and the child will not be able to access them as memories. In the classroom, they may appear to be following along, but when it's time for them to recall anything the content is gone. This will not appear to bother them. They will seem fairly placid. But think of the sulfurous hot spots found in areas of the earth with a lot of thermal activity. Eventually that sulphur will explode, and so will these children. It may be an explosion of temper or of mischief, but they will explode. Alice is a good example of a child with too much sulphur.

Steiner says that if you are working with a child with black hair it's possible that they have too much iron, and that when you are working with a child with blond or reddish hair you have the possibility of a sulphur condition. But, if you imagine two people with black hair sitting in front of a window with the sunlight streaming in behind them, you might notice that one of them has blue highlights to their hair and the other has some reddish mahogany lights.

It is possible for a person with black hair to have too much sulphur. You may be working with a child with blondish hair, but have the experience every night as you recall that child in you meditation that the child's hair always appears to you as darker than it truly is. You might sometimes notice that this child has iron tendencies.

These conditions affect the child all the way down to their physical body. The iron child may need sulphur as a medicine. They may need to avoid iron rich foods. The sulphur child may need more iron and need to avoid foods with too much sulphur.

The last set of polarities is also more static. In the first of these we have a difficulty where the physical body is so dense that the astral/ego cannot penetrate properly. In German, Steiner refers to these children as *schwachsinnig*. This could be translated literally as "weak-sensed."* Another way to refer to this polarity is "underactive."

Here you have a child who understands everything you are asking of them. They understand, but they cannot get their will to engage enough to do what you are asking them to do. Steiner speaks of us all coming to this earth with all the thoughts we need already present. This is really one of the pillars of Waldorf Education: the assumption that we are working with the word "educate" literally, from its Latin origin meaning to draw out. He says there are really very few true defects of intellect; rather, there are defects of the will. In the underactive child this can be seen very clearly. Peter is an example of a child who could be seen as underactive.

The underactive child's body may appear too dense. It may appear too doughy or floppy. The body weighs too heavily on this child's soul and so they can have real feelings of melancholy.

Again we can have the opposite condition. Here, the body doesn't wait for the ego at all. It takes off on it's own without any guidance from the ego. The physical is not strong enough, so the astral overwhelms it. Steiner refers to this as the "manic" child. Without Curative Education they may well become manic later in life. For now, we can speak of them as being "overactive."

---

* In the 1972 English version of *Curative Education* this term was rendered "feeble-minded" (an echo of 1 Thessalonians 5:14 [KJV]), while in the latest translation (A. Meuss, 2014) *schwachsinnig Kinder* are "children with learning difficulties."

This condition is a picture of the "chicken with its head cut off." The limbs are never waiting for a command from the thinking. It may begin with the legs being constantly in motion. The hands will seem compelled to grasp at things randomly. Their mouth may follow suit and never be still or quiet. Their heads can become packed with too many ideas, what can be described as "mind confetti." When you are telling a story or bringing an idea into your Main Lesson, they will need to constantly interrupt to interject something that may or may not be related to the subject at hand. When they attempt to put their thoughts on paper, they will get so lost in the web of their own thinking that very little will make it to the page. They may be gifted at mental math, so much so that the assumption is made that they are brilliant mathematicians. But, as with writing, they will rarely be able to solve math problems on paper. They will fill pages in their math books with diagrams and charts and addenda of their own creation, but little of this will be relevant, and in the end the problem will not be solved correctly.

Think about Max. If a child like this is not helped, it is easy to see how such a brilliant person could grow up unable to achieve anything worthy of their capacity. Steiner says that the potential for violence is there if the child isn't helped.

All of these conditions can be present in the same child to varying degrees. You will find that when you first start to work with the child you may need to address what seems to be the most glaring difficulty, but then, as the healing begins, you will uncover new layers requiring you to look at the child through the lens of a different aspect of one of these polarities. It's like peeling an onion.

Steiner talks about using our sense of smell as a tool for discrimination. We can learn to "smell" the differences in the polarities at any given time. A child may not do something. We can "smell" if this seeming reluctance has to do with the fear of the thin-skinned moment, the indifference of the sulphur experience, or the frustration of the underactive child who understands what you want her to do but can't engage her will.

"Thick-skinnedness," iron, or underactiveness may have too strong of a connection to gravity. "Thin-skinnedness," sulphur, or overactive may be too strongly situated in levity. We may experience too much contraction or too much expansion. All of these things are clues.

Rudolf Steiner has given us these pictures of the curative polarities as nourishment. With breathing, we make a connection between the outer world and ourselves. With warmth, we create the space within us where we can feel ourselves as something existing independently from the outer world. We are given a place within us that is ready to receive. With nourishing, we begin to fill that space within us. These pictures Steiner gave us are a gift. We don't have to reinvent the wheel; we have a basic framework to begin our own approach.

Karl König connects "nourishing" to the sense of sight. He says that both of these are connected to the light. This is difficult to understand until he reminds us that, in former times, all of our nourishment came from the light. He calls it the cosmic nutrition stream. We still receive "nourishment" from this stream through the "light" that illuminates the world for us when we touch it through our senses. The "light" of our perceptions enters into us as food for our souls. We bring these impressions into us as memories. When we observe the children, and bring those images into the warmth of our inner being, we can then begin to illuminate our understanding through the light of the pictures of the polarities.

Breathing, warming, and nourishing are the end of the first phase of the life processes. These first three processes are given to us. At the next step, "secreting," we have to begin to give back. Something has to come from us.

Here we come to a danger point.

If we don't begin to work with what we are given as nourishment it will become a mere deposit. It will become something we deposit in our souls and let turn into "fat." Unless we begin to bring something of ourselves to these pictures of the polarities they will become "fat" within us. "Thick-skinned," "thin-skinned," "iron," sulphur," "underactive," and "overactive" will become yet another set of words we throw about without working at their meaning. They will become labels just like "autism," "ADHD," or "dyslexia" and we will throw them around so that we sound like we know what we are talking about without having to dig deeper, truly understand, and do something. We will become fat and lazy in our understanding.

In *A Living Physiology*, König describes a phenomenon he has observed in the children he worked with. He says:

> Usually, if the ego is too strongly engaged in depositing, the following occurs. These children are nice, pleasant, well-adapted and cheerful, and we expect they will develop well if they come to Camphill, but when they come we gradually discover that in spite of whatever we do for them they remain the same [...] Such a child remains completely static for the following reason. The powers of memory are there, but they work in the wrong place. What is called *die Merkfaehigkeit* in German, the ability to mark or note down, is not available to them because the power of depositing binds all and everything that is memory. Therefore such a child "remembers," so to speak, his fat, but he does not remember his lessons. (p. 90)

We may find it "nice, pleasant, and cheerful" to throw around terms like "thick-skinned" or "thin-skinned." We might start neatly sorting the children we work with into "nice, pleasant, and cheerful" boxes built out of a superficial understanding and feel that we have done something. We haven't. The pictures of the polarities are a starting point. Now we have to get to work. We have to engage ourselves and begin to digest this food that Steiner has given us. We have to look at the next step, which is "secreting," meaning the beginning of digestion and truly tasting what we have been given.

4. SECRETING

The pictures of the polarities that Steiner has given are foundation for our understanding. They are our base camp, but now, as we move into the fourth step in working with the life processes, we come to a place where we have to bring something of ourselves to the work. In chapter two we talked about the gift that the pedagogical law can be for us when we use the contents of our own biography to build a little "hut" of understanding within ourselves: A place where we can begin to think with our heart. When we take this understanding and begin to overlay it with the pictures of the polarities we come to a place where we can feel our way into the child's experience through allowing it to resonate within our own experience. We experience the world through our senses. Steiner talks about at least twelve ways we can experience the outer world. He talks about several more when we begin to experience the spiritual world, but for now talking about the twelve is enough.

Each of the twelve senses brings us a different potential for experience. Steiner says that the first sense, *touch*, resonates through all of our senses. We can make a picture of each sense as a paradigm. We can make a watermark as to the widest range of experience possible through each sense, but we also have to look at how each sense might be curtailed or shadowed because of the conditions of the polarities. None of this curtailing or shadowing needs to become a permanent condition, but when we are beginning to work at a healing process we have to look at these darker pictures in order to really understand the inner life of the child we are working with, and we have to look at them through the lens of our own emotional and sensory experiences.

When we began to talk about the polarities, we started by talking about the lemniscate of the four bodies. Steiner talks about the lemniscate of the ego, astral, etheric, and physical bodies as an image of the prototype out of which the bodies should be working together. The condition of the polarities comes about when that prototype is somehow not in balance, and when this lemniscate is not in balance it will have a direct effect on the child's ability to experience the world through his or her senses. Remember that ideally we should be able to sense our ego not only in the quiet and calm behind our third eye, but also in the warmth element that surrounds us in our limbs. The organ that surrounds us, that forms our container, is our skin. Ideally our ego would take up residence in this container, giving us a living experience of where we end and where the world begins, but when we are looking at the experience of the polarities we have to understand that the ego is not able to come to the right kind of communication with our skin. Either the astral/ego is trapped too far inside our organism, as it is in the thick-skinned condition, or it has leaked too far outside our container (thin-skinned). With the iron/sulphur and overactive/underactive polarities there are also difficulties with the placement of the ego/astral that prevent the ego from forming its proper relationship with our container, the skin. The skin is the organ for the first of our twelve senses, the sense of touch. Beginning with the sense of touch we are going to go through all of the senses, first making a picture of the sense with its ideal potential and then looking at how it might be curtailed or shadowed because of the condition of the polarities.

Touch

We normally think of "touch" as an experience of texture, but when Steiner speaks of the sense of touch he does not mean tactile differentiation. He means "touch" as an experience of boundary, a knowing of where we end and where the world begins. Ideally, our first experience of touch should be our birth. We are touched all over when we pass through the birth canal. After our time of free floating in the womb we emerge into the outer world with a tactual awakening of every inch of our being. We are born. We have arrived on the earth. We have our first lesson in the experience of boundary, our own boundary, which is the container of our skin.

The sense of touch tells us where we are, makes us aware of our own existence, and out of that certainty we can approach the world.

We can "touch" the world through all of our senses. It can be found in the quality of our listening and in the directness of our gaze. It is the capacity that allows us to perceive and understand others. We can "touch" the world when we smell it or taste it. We know we are warm or cold through a kind of touch. The longing to touch is a darkened or unconscious facility of our will, a capacity that can motivate the soul.

Through the sense of touch we form memory. As we pass through the world we are taking in impressions by "touching" the world with our senses. We then "digest" those impressions in a manner that enables us to recall them through memory. If you think of where you were an hour previous to reading these words you will recall impressions you took in at that time. Maybe you were cooking something, or driving home, or petting your dog. The smells, tastes, sights, sounds and textures of those experiences were taken in to your unconscious through an ability of your sense of touch, and so now you can bring them back as a memory. Our memories are like a blanket of thoughts that surround us. They give us a feeling of certainty. We know we existed, that we "were" an hour ago because we can bring back the memories from that time as proof. These things we remember are like a shrine of our existence. They confirm the spiritual reality of our being, our ending and beginning place. To know "touch" is to know the "I Am."

Through touch a human being meets and makes her relationship to the outer world. It is an expression of our boundary, our bodily existence. It allows us to feel the reality of our earthly existence. "Touch" can mirror for us reality without the forming of judgment, and so can provide moments of free interchange between the world and ourselves. With our birth we begin a new chapter in our earthly biographies, temporarily leaving our cosmic home behind. As we "touch" the world through our senses and take in the beauty around us, we are consoled for having to leave the beauty of the cosmos.

"Touch" makes it possible for us not to meld with everything around us. We can become more than a small drop in the cosmic sea. "Touch" provides us the ability to separate, and that is what allows us to form self-consciousness. "Touch" is a knock on the door that opens to invite us into self-awareness. Through "touch" we separate and connect simultaneously. "Touch" is the mediator of communication with the world that enables us to have the courage to exist.

When a child is "stuck" in one of the conditions of the polarities, his or her sense of touch will be compromised. Again, this does not need to be a permanent condition, but it is the place the child is often in when we first meet them, and so we need to understand it. When the primal boundary of "touch" has been compromised, the child cannot feel certain of his or her own existence. This makes it extremely difficult for them to live. This is a child who lives in a constant state of fear: this is the first thing we have to understand. When we think about Jasper, and his continual stream of frustrating behavior, we have to first understand that he in living in constant fear. This is why seeing him as a "choleric" run amok is such a disservice to him. His behavior has a context that we will never truly understand until we see his actions as a reaction to the fear he experiences all the time. Fear has two responses: fight or flight. With Jasper we see something of the fight response. With Sienna we see someone who is acting out of flight.

When a child is struggling to build up a sense of touch, his or her emotional life will overwhelm them constantly without there being any discernible manifesting causes. Feelings and memories will fly about them, like leaves in a whirlwind. Without a sense of touch to bring meaning and continuity to their memories, they will not be able to contextualize those memories. Memories and feelings that may have been relevant years ago can surface at times when they are no longer appropriate. This can be really frustrating for parents and teachers because, without an understanding of the child's inner condition, the adult will perceive the child as lying. For example, a child may have had surgery at a very young age. The pain and the fear of the surgery may have created some "thin-skinnedness" in that child. The child has a memory of surgical masks, but she can't put that memory into context, and now she has a panicked response to anyone in a mask. We may get frustrated with her. We may try to reason with her. We won't begin to make any progress until we understand the extent of the fear she is feeling.

Any child in this condition is at the mercy of emotions they cannot name or contain. They don't know what to do. Their heart will race, they are full of uncertainty and they don't know where to turn because there is no external cause for their distress. This then is a child who will go to great lengths to feel anything, because that will at least temporarily assuage the feeling of fear. In a thick-skinned moment the child will hurt others. It will not be personal, and there may not be any perceivable catalyst for their behavior, but in that moment of making strong contact with something outside of themselves the child will know where his or her skin is located. In the moment they, at least temporarily, find their skin, the fear is abated: "Here I am." They may not feel the pain the strong contact has caused them, but they will feel the temporary relief from fear.

In a thin-skinned moment the child will do things to hurt her- or himself. They may bang their head against a wall, or hit themselves with a fist. They may cut or burn themselves. These actions are often misinterpreted as suicidal gestures. These are not suicidal actions, but more like the opposite. These are desperate attempts to feel something, to gain assurance of one's own existence, in order to find, at least temporarily, the courage to get through the next few minutes.

Sense of Life

The sense of life is built out of the sense of touch. Karl König gives us the following picture.[*] He says to imagine our sense of touch as the shore of a lake. Our sense of life is the water within the shore. Is the surface of the lake smooth and placid, or is it choppy and stormy? Once we know that we are, we can begin to ask *how* we are. Our sense of life alerts us to pain, hunger, or sickness. It tells us when we are too tired, too hot, or too cold. It also can provide us with the feeling of contentment when all is well within us. The organ for the sense of touch is our sympathetic and parasympathetic nervous systems, whose branches literally form a "Tree of Life" within us. This is the sense that tell us that our body is ours. We are the being living within the container of our skin. We are an eternal being, who once had a home in the spiritual world, and

---

[*] See "The Sense of Touch and the Sense of Life" in *A Living Physiology*.

will have again, but for now we have an earthly home within the confines of our body. This is what allows our body to become a temple for our spirit.

When our sense of life is not in order we cannot yet form a right relationship to our body. "Contact disturbances," what people like to refer to now as "the autism spectrum" is simply the result of a sense of life that has not yet been fully awakened. When we begin to understand this, and begin to work with the sense of life and all the other senses, particularly the lower four, we will have come a long way toward helping the child to overcome these difficulties. No one who understands Steiner's work in Curative Education would use the term "autistic spectrum." When we put the label to the behavior we think we understand, we are working contrary to Steiner's intentions in Curative Education and will be placing a large stumbling block in our way towards healing this child. "Autistic spectrum," or any other label we choose to place on the child, is an example of what Steiner calls "a conclusion that people come to that are so very confused." We will begin to do "God knows what," as Steiner puts it, and, as he says, this will ultimately destroy the genius in the child. He goes further to say, "the first thing the doctor or teacher has to do is reject the application of criterion and get beyond the stage of making pronouncements as to what is clever or reasonable, in accordance with the habits of thought that prevail today."*

When the child has yet to develop a sense of life, their own body feels to them as "it." This is a child who does not identify his or her own body as belonging to his or her own self. It is just something they are forced to carry around. They may feel just as connected to any other inanimate object around them as they do to their own body. He or she may feel much more connected to others than to themselves. If you ask this child how they are feeling they will respond with how they intuit you to be feeling. Asking them about themselves feels like a trick question. If they don't feel that they live in their own body, how should they know how it feels in there?

Because this child does not live in his or her body they may feel offended if you try to look for them in there. When you look them

---

*   See Lecture One of *The Curative Education Course*.

in the eyes, you are not looking at where they feel themselves to be. They may feel more "seen" when you look slightly away from them. The child who is still working to develop a sense of life may not respond to their own name, because he or she doesn't yet identify that name with himself or herself. They have yet to have the "I" experience we have come to expect at around age three. This child may have difficulty speaking. They may be choosing not to speak, not because they can't, but because they have yet to discover a reason to speak. They may not make enough of a connection to the outer world to feel the need to name the things around them, and when the child doesn't begin to use speech in the right way it becomes more difficult for thinking to develop.

Our sense of life should tell us when we are cold, tired, sick, or hungry. Without it, the child is not aware of these things and may behave in ways that give us a contrary picture to the reality. In the evening, for example, the more tired the child is, the more active they may become. They may become quite frantic. We may surmise that they're not tired at all and keep them up even later. This is why it is so important that a child working on developing his or her own sense of life has a regular bedtime. We have to provide the outer structure for this child so that he or she can begin to form one inwardly. If bedtime is consistent and appropriate, the child will begin to identify the feeling they have at their bedtime as "tired" and will accept going to bed more and more readily.

The same thing goes for "sick," "hungry," and "cold." These are things the child doesn't know on their own. Often the sick child will be sent to school because "they were so active in the morning I thought they must be okay." The child becomes more active when they are sick because, despite not having developed their sense of life enough to know the feeling they have means they are sick, they do feel enough to be restless. They become more active in a misguided attempt to escape the uncomfortability they feel when they are sick. If the child has a fever, a very runny nose, or a bad cough they are sick. Sick children need to stay home, in bed, and rest. They need tea and stories. In this way they will begin to listen more to their bodies and begin to learn how to care for themselves.

A child who is working on the sense of life will not be able to identify the rumbly feeling in their tummy as "hungry." The hungrier they get, the more they may turn down food. If we try to bribe them to eat by offering them only things we know will get their attention, things like chicken nuggets or macaroni and cheese, they will learn that they need only eat those few things they are fond of and can avoid even trying foods that are not on their very short lists. They will become picky and unhealthy eaters. Mealtimes need to be consistent so that the child can begin to notice that the feeling they have in their tummy at mealtime means they are hungry. They should be given a variety of foods so that their taste buds can begin to wake up and develop. As adults we may chose to be vegetarian or vegan, but Steiner says that children who are working on their will do need meat and dairy in their diets.

This child will also most likely not be aware of when they are cold. They don't feel the cold because they are not in their bodies. The more they are excarnated, the less chance they have to develop a healthy sense of life. Children need to be appropriately dressed in order for them to begin to experience being in their body and on the earth as a cozy and good place to be.

The body should be the mediator between the soul and the world in which the soul is living. König says that without the sense of life as mediator the body stands between the soul and the world and eclipses it, just as the moon stands before the sun during an eclipse. When this child is moved from a familiar environment, this can cause them to feel so disoriented that they are no longer certain who they are for a while. This is why transitions can be so difficult. Assimilating anything is very difficult. These children are alone, no matter how many people are around them. They live in a state of constant terror. They are isolated behind an invisible wall where they may begin to hallucinate. König says they are at risk for schizophrenia later in life.

Sense of (One's Own) Movement

Our bodies should contain their own geography. Where is our left little finger? Our right knee? Can we find our way within ourselves? Are we aware of each corner of our internal country, and cognizant of it as we move through space? Awareness of our movement is what makes us human. A machine is not aware that it moves. Without awareness of movement there can be no healthy movement, and so movements appear to be random and senseless. It is the sense of one's own movement that gives sense to one's own movements. The muscles are the organs for this sense. Our sense of our own movement reaches into all of our movements, from sitting and standing to running and hopping. It also supports all of our academic learning. Everything we learn has a basis in movement. To follow the shape of the letter "B" we first have to know about up and down and right and left. We need movement to understand the form of a sentence, paragraph, or essay. Every math process involves inwardly tracking the movement of the math problem. This is why it's so important to teach math based in movement and not merely connect it with abstract fictive characters, like "Prince Plus" or "Princess Times." When we add or multiply we are moving forward in space on a number line. When we subtract or divide we are moving backward on that number line. True movements are the foundation for understanding. Movement helps the forms of the outer world resonate within oneself.

The ability to follow instructions is part of the sense of our own movement. If I were to say, "stop reading, stand up, turn around three times, clap your hands, and then sit down again," you would first have to make an inner picture of these instructions so that you could understand them and carry them through outwardly.

The sense of our own movement gives us our sense of freedom, both in our bodies and in our souls. We can control space. As we master the possibilities of the movements our bodies we feel joy. Joy is a gift of the awareness of the sense of movement. It comes from mastering something with effort and sweat. Often a baby's first smile is connected to his or her first awareness of his or her own movement.

Our sense of movement also enables us to have a sense for the movement of our own life story, our biography. It can give us a sense for the direction we should take in life, the ability to discern the essential. This is the sense of grace we feel when we are on the right path. We can make a goal and follow it through. This is the sense at work when we feel we are going in the right direction in life, the direction we have chosen for ourselves, the place our life is calling us to. After we die, when we look back on our life, if we can see the pattern and beauty of our life path, we have this sense of our own movement to thank for that.

When the sense of movement is not in order the child can feel no joy. Running, skipping, and playing become meaningless activities. This is then the child who can create difficulties on the playground because they are not able to perceive meaning in the movements of the game. To them, the game appears random, and so they try to enter in randomly, which disturbs the play in ways that others mistake for willful destructiveness. The child is not able to live into the movement of the game outwardly and so they cannot recreate those movements inwardly, where they could translate them into something meaningful. Without the ability to form movements outwardly they cannot be formed inwardly. This will result in great academic difficulties. The child will be unable to follow the movement intrinsic in all academic work. This is exacerbated when the teacher works with "copy off the board" in his or her classroom. The child realizes that copying what the teacher has put on the board should be an easy task, but in the transition from seeing the material to be copied on the board and then turning his or her attention to the blank page in the Main Lesson Book, the form, the movement of the material is lost. Children like Jasper, who are in reality very intelligent children, will be frustrated to the point of breaking their pencils, tearing up their Main Lesson Books, or throwing things because they know they should be able to do such an easy task, but can't. They will begin to think they are stupid. Their self-esteem plummets and they will act out in a desperate attempt to get someone to help them. Because their behavior is not likely to be perceived by their teacher as a cry for help, but instead as purposefully disruptive, they will be sent out of the classroom clearly feeling they have been "bad." They will begin to see themselves as bad, as well as stupid, and their self-image will plummet even further.

You will observe difficulties with the sense of one's own movement in the classroom too. Children will sit on one leg or wrap their ankles around the legs of their chair. They will situate their work at an odd angle to their desk and you might notice that, even if they are writing with their right hand, they have positioned their head so that their left eye can be used to see the page more strongly than their right eye. These are ways of communicating to you their need for movement work. The temptation is to address these things as symptoms and to offer them accommodations or special equipment. These things will not solve the problem but will make the child feel even more inadequate.

Without a sense of their own movement the children do not have a way to orient themselves in their own body geography. They will be confused by very simple things like asking them to move to the right or left or come towards you or backup. They will not have established a dominant side, either right-sided or left-sided. You will be able to observe in their movement that they have not yet completed the tasks of the first year of life. They have either not overcome gravity enough, or they might be stuck in a place of too much levity. They have not yet brought consciousness to the reflex to expand or contract their limbs. When you watch them walk and run you will see that the three planes of movement; right/left, above/below and forward/backward are not in sync. Their movement will appear jerky or uncoordinated.

In the child who is in a thick-skinned condition, you will see movements that are gravity bound, jerky, random and disorganized. If the child is in a thin-skinned condition their movement will be loose. They may "puddle" onto the person next to them or that person's desk. You will sense their hesitancy.

When the child is struggling with their sense of movement it will be very hard for them to follow instructions. They will hear you just fine, they will most likely really want to comply, but they lack the ability to form an inner picture of the instructions you give, so they will be unable to outwardly follow and carry out what you have asked them to do.

Because part of the sense of movement is the ability to make an intention and follow it through, this child will have a very difficult time with completion. They may grow up to be an adult who cannot make a commitment. They start new things with great enthusiasm only to lose interest. They may move from job to job, always blaming the situation for their own inability to remain long term. They will begin to lose the sense that their life has meaning. They may look for outside sources such as alcohol or drugs, even prescription drugs, to mask the feeling of emptiness in their life.

Sense of Balance

The organ for the sense of balance is located in the labyrinth of our inner ear. This is what allows us to experience gravity and space. This is the place where we can sense ourselves at inner rest, the kind of quiet inner rest that allows us to move with consciousness. This is the compass for orienting ourselves within our body geography. It is what brings certitude as to the location of right/left, forward/backward, and up/down within the container of our skin. This compass not only orients us within our own bodies, our own inner space, it also allows us to orient ourselves in the outer world through our sense perceptions. This is how we form a consciousness of the world, and how we can come to harmony with our environment. We have a relationship with the world thanks to our sense of balance.

The ability to have the feeling for self-continuity is part of the sense of balance, connected also to the sense of life. If you know that when you leave one room and enter another you still are you, or if you know when you wake up in the morning you are still the same person you were the night before, you have your sense of balance to thank for that. This is an experience of our own ego. The first time we experience this in our life is the moment when, as a very young child, we stood in balance unaided. We have come to balance. In our feet and our legs we feel physical balance and gravity. Our arms and our hands, which are now able to move freely, allow us to feel soul balance. In that space within our heads, navigating the inner ear, where we feel ourselves at quiet, calm, peace, and rest we experience spiritual balance. This is where our I, that spiritual core of our being, can begin to express itself through thinking and speaking. This is where we form individual consciousness.

It is within this place of quiet that we can take in speech and allow it to resonate within us so that we can distill meaning. This is what is meant when people speak of "auditory processing." When we take in the sounds we hear in speech as a very young child, into this quiet space within us where they can resonate, we are then able to replicate them in our own speech.

Part of our sense of balance allows us to be present in a large space and not feel overwhelmed. It allows us to stand at the edge of a precipice and not experience vertigo. We can hold ourselves inwardly in balance with our ego and allow our etheric body to travel to the periphery of the space around us like a buttress supporting us in uprightness so we don't lose our balance.

The sense of balance, working in soul balance and spiritual balance, is an immediate expression of our own being. When we are working within the confines of our higher self we are in soul and spiritual balance. We can then orient ourselves within the world of our emotions without tipping too far in any one direction. We come to this out of our own inner quiet. Out of this we can form our own opinions and viewpoints. We learn to know ourselves.

When the sense of balance is not in order we never come to inner calm and quiet. A child may do several things to try to compensate for this. They may rock in their chair, or sit tipped on two legs or even one. This is an attempt to try to stimulate the inner ear so that they feel a facsimile of balance. They may make their own "white noise" to try to mask the noise in their heads.

When these children are made to sit on a one-legged stool because they cannot sit still it may superficially make things easier for the teacher. The child may be so taken up with not falling off that they appear to be stiller and less of a distraction in the classroom. If you observe this child from the back of the room you will see all sorts of convulsions going on with their legs in order to stay upright. These stools are a band-aid, but they do nothing to address the root difficulties.

Because the child who is working on the sense of balance does not carry the knowledge that they are the same person in one place as they are in another, transitions will be very difficult for them. Every time you ask them to move from one location to another, you are erasing their sense of self. They literally do not know who they are for a while. This is very disorienting. Knowing that when they sleep they will wake up without this sense of self can be a reason the child resists falling asleep at night.

When the physical body cannot come to balance rightly the soul and spirit will struggle with balance as well. You will see this in how the child overreacts to seemingly benign situations. They may have large meltdowns or act out aggressively and not be able afterwards to acknowledge their responsibility for these actions.

A large classroom, one with perhaps more than thirty children, will be very overwhelming for the child who is working to have a sense of balance. The size of the room itself will feel like too much space for this child to fill out of his or her etheric body. They will not feel held or contained and this will make it very easy for them to get "out of themselves." Because they do not yet have a peaceful space within themselves to come into when they need to comprehend things they will be very distracted. They may react with too much sensitivity or too much irritability (depending on whether they are in a thin- or thick-skinned moment) to the noise of others because they may perceive that noise as being made deliberately just to annoy them. They may begin to create noise of their own to retaliate.

When the child has struggled with balance since the beginning of their life they will not yet have had the experience of that calmness and quiet in their inner ear. Because of this, their speech will be affected. They will not yet have had the opportunity to truly hear the sounds of speech and to let those sounds resonate within their own inner quiet. When they cannot truly hear the sounds it is really difficult for them to replicate them. Once we understand that speech difficulties are really balance difficulties we will be a long way down the path towards giving these children the support they really need.

Children who are not able to develop their own sense of balance will struggle to form their own opinions. They will easily live into the thoughts and feelings of others at the cost of their own individuality. If they never learn to keep their emotional balance in a range that reflects their own higher self König says that, as adults, they may be at risk for "bipolar" type conditions. They may long for quiet and inner peace, but not be able to find it. Suicide may seem to be the only way they will ever come to rest.

Sense of Smell

With the sense of smell we cross over from the lower to the higher senses. Our sense of smell is involuntary. When we breathe we are compelled to smell things. It is perhaps our most sensitive sense. Smells can overpower us, and we can get lost in them. They carry memory with them and can take us back to events in the past. Things can smell good, and they can smell bad. The ability to discern this is connected to our ability to make moral distinctions. In this way "smell" can be an education in good and evil. Our physical sense of smell is connected with our olfactory gland. It is connected with our old life of instinct. As we begin to transform ourselves into beings with more of a spiritual potential we also transform the olfactory gland into something capable of helping us to evolve spiritually. The location of our olfactory gland is the same as the location of our third eye, our "two-petaled lotus flower."* This is the lotus of differentiation; the ability to sense good and evil spiritually. Hopefully, as we mature, we learn to sit with our decisions long enough to "smell" them. We can learn to discern whether or not our decisions smell good or bad, and this can become an inner compass pointing toward correct choices as we try to intuit our life path. This is a very important capacity for teachers to develop. Steiner never tells us what to do. He is always clear we must work on ourselves so that we can become a vessel for correct understandings. He leaves it to us to make Waldorf Education, of which Curative Education is meant to be a part, into something artistic and fluid that demands our own creative initiative. An evolved sense of smell can tell us whether our creative ideas are on the right track or not.

The sense of smell should also lead us toward perceiving the innate goodness or evilness of situations we meet in life. Materialism can be found everywhere, even in things which purport to be spiritual. Our sense of smell can be honed to feel the real intent behind the rhetoric and can then help us to sidestep things that would otherwise hinder us from following our intended path. We

---

* See Rudolf Steiner, *How to Know Higher Worlds,* Chapter 4, "Some Results of Initiation."

can begin to feel the healthiness in the etheric body surrounding someone or something and that can help us to know when we need to tread lightly and work even more strongly out of our own I. A portion of our own I lives in this space, and it can help us to recognize where the I of the world is working. The future of humanity hangs on our ability to form these capacities. König says this is where the battle between moral and non-moral forces begins; in the ability to discriminate.

When we are working with children within the pictures of the polarities, we will see how these conditions affect the senses. A child in a thick-skinned condition might be impervious to smell. They may find pleasure in things most of us find repulsive, such as the smell of cess. This will have a direct correlation to this child's ability to form moral distinctions. They will struggle to understand what is so wrong in seemingly aggressive actions toward another when they perceive that other to be in their way.

The child in the thin-skinned condition may have an encyclopedic memory for smell. They may react to all smells as if they are bad. They may imagine smells that aren't there. They too will have difficulty making moral distinctions. They will perceive ill intent where none exists. Little things may take on too much significance. They may imagine insults and injuries and get very angry when these events aren't taken seriously. They might feel "bullied" when in fact the only thing keeping them from belonging within the group is their own oversensitivity to things that most likely are not completely real.

With both these extremes the child will need support to stay within a place of balance. They will need help to begin to develop enough moral differentiation skills to stay grounded in what is true.

Sense of Taste

With the sense of taste comes choice. We can chose whether or not we will taste something. This is a sense we have much more when we are a baby. The infant tastes with his or her whole body. The baby wiggles with delight when something tastes good and shudders with disgust when it does not. We lose the force of this experience as we age.

When we taste something we are having an intimate conversation with it. The experience we can have when we really take in the nature of something through taste is an experience bordering on clairvoyance. Taste is a kind of union of the senses of touch, life, and warmth. We should be able to tell if something is healthy for us or not through our sense of taste. When we eat foods that are processed and full of chemicals we lose this ability; we become less able to tell if something is false in what we are eating.

Different aspects of taste can enliven our soul's experience. Salt is connected with thinking capacities. Sour things wake us up. Sweet things give us a feeling of contentment, and a little bit of what is bitter can stir up our will. Without small amounts of bitter foods in their diets children will not develop strength. This is true literally and metaphorically. Children need to experience all four aspects of taste to enliven the different taste buds located on different areas of their tongues. If their tongue is allowed to be too sleepy because the child only wants certain kinds of foods and is allowed to indulge those preferences the child may have a more difficult time using their tongues to form speech. If they are not able to create a range of sounds, they may not be able to recreate those sounds inwardly, so they may have a harder time learning to connect the sounds with symbols and this could slow down their ability to read.

We speak of words as being bitter or sweet. Words can poison us. A person can have good taste or bad taste. The group consciousness behind these delineations is what forms our ideas of culture.

When the child is still struggling to develop his or her sense of taste they may develop certain eating disorders. When the child is in a thick-skinned condition they may eat copious amounts of food. They will eat it so fast they will not taste it. They are not eating to experience flavors, or because they are hungry; they are eating as rapidly as they can because, when their bellies are full, they can feel where they are for a while. It is the same impulse that might make them want to crash and bump into things. In the moment they feel that strong contact they locate themselves and have some respite from the fear of not knowing where they end and where the world begins. Eating so much and so fast may result in the child voiding what they have eaten before they have had time to truly digest it. Their bodies will then not be able to assimilate the nutritional value they might otherwise get from their food. This child may hoard or steal food. They may become very agitated when others are served, even if their own plates are full. They may be afraid that others will get something that they feel should belong to them. They cannot bear to leave the table if there is still food sitting there.

The child in a thin-skinned condition perceives food only as texture. They do not like many textures, so many foods will elicit a gag reflex. They may not like to have the various foods touching on their plate, or they may like to eat just one thing at a time, or they may only eat foods of a certain color. Because they are so used to being outside of their bodies, they may not find the feeling of a full belly pleasant. They won't like that feeling that tells them they are related to their own body, that they live there. This can become an addiction to the feeling of being empty or "light," which they perceive as being good. This is part of the picture of anorexia.

Sense of Sight

Seeing is a kind of touching. Our eyes are, in a way, a kind of limb, and with them we can reach out and touch the world. When we really look at someone, really see them, we are touching them with our eyes. The cosmos comes to meet us through sight. The cosmos meets us with the light of the sun that it lends to our eyes. Without the sun we could not see. The eye is the child of the sun, and seeing is a way out of the dark well of our inner being. By using the limb of our sight to reach out and touch a focal point ahead of us we are better able to come to balance. In the autobiography of Jacques Lusseyran, the blind hero of the French Resistance[*] he tells us that to reach out to the world with our eyes and take it in means to love the world. In the book *Nature Spirits and What They Tell Say: Interviews with Verena Holstein,*[†] we are told that the gnomes and the spirits of the forest are helped every time we really look at a tree. This can help to heal the forest.

When a child is in a thick-skinned condition or a thin-skinned condition this may cause them to perceive the world differently

---

[*] Jacques Lusseyran, *And There Was Light* (Floris Books, 1990).
[†] Wolfgang Weirauch, Ed. (Floris Books, 2005).

than others. With a thick-skinned condition the child may remain stuck so deeply within their own skin that they don't use the limbs of their eyes well enough to really take in what they are seeing. Physically they may see just fine, but they may not register what they have seen until they crash into it. This is in part why they may crash into others and then blame them. When you are teaching this child to read you may notice that they read the end of the word first. Reading may be difficult for them because they don't get the connection between looking at the page and reading.

These children may also have a hard time understanding the social significance of looking at the person you are talking to. This can make conversations difficult. You may be talking to another child, someone not even in their vicinity, and they will react (with great irritation) as if you were talking to them. You may have even called the other child by name. It won't help. You will have to spell out for them first that you did not say their name; you said someone else's name. You may have to remind them that they are Jasper, so when I say Max I do not mean Jasper. Then you will have to point out that you were not looking in their direction. If you had meant to speak to them you would have looked at them. You may need to repeat this conversation several times a day.

When the child is in a thin-skinned condition they may see everything literally from a bird's eye view. Because of this they may be able to have some perceptions of what happens behind them, or even in another room. Because they do not live in their body, they do not experience the world horizontally. If a child has ever drawn you a picture in which a tree looked like an oddly shaped green blob you may have seen a picture drawn by a child who experiences the world in this way. Because they have to "translate" everything from a vertical point of view to a horizontal one, things that would normally be simple become much more complicated. In order to catch a beanbag they first have to translate what they see from above to what they can anticipate coming at them horizontally. The extra moments it takes to do this is enough to miss the timing necessary to catch the beanbag. When children reverse letters and numbers it is often because of the difficulty they have moving from the plane in which they perceive to the plane they need to write in. You will notice that when the child begins to heal and becomes more at home in his or her body this difficulty will go away. You will know you have arrived when you ask the child to go over their work and correct the things that are written not quite correctly and they can tell immediately which letters or numbers they need to fix.

Due to difficulties in perceiving horizontal space, this child may have a hard time with a direction such as "move to the left." Usually the child is well aware that they have to do extra work to make the world make sense to them, and this will make them much more easily frustrated.

A child who is working on their sense of sight, combined with a difficulty with the sense of life may develop a "fixed" gaze. They may do this to hold themselves steady from their "bird's-eye-view" of the world, or they may do it because the world causes them too much pain. They may learn that when they fix their gaze on a certain point they can use this gaze to form a kind of thread that will help to lead them even further out of their bodies, far enough to be completely shut off from the world. They will do this to remove themselves from an experience that is painful or fearful for them.

Sense of Warmth

The sense of warmth lies at the doorway between our higher and our highest senses. Our sense of warmth connects with our sense of balance, allowing for own bodily warmth to stay in a stable relationship with that of our surroundings. The sense of warmth and the sense of balance work together in many ways within our bodies. As well as keeping our body temperature constant, they work together to keep the mineral content of our blood constant. They help to maintain the rhythm of our circulation and breathing.

Remember the lemniscate of the four bodies? In our head our ego is the innermost part of ourselves, but in the metabolic-limb system the ego is the outermost element. This is because the ego is able to travel through our bloodstream, surrounding us with the warmth of our own ego. This is part of the reason it is important to dress the children we are working with overly warmly. While they are working to strengthen and develop their senses they need the extra skin that extra layers of clothing can give them. This can help them to begin to sense the warmth of their ego protecting them and making their own bodies someplace good to live in. Warmth was our primordial condition, and it is still something we need in order to live. When we are holding the children within our ego they need to feel it surrounding them with our warmth. True ego presence is never cold. When it becomes cold and brittle it is because we have slipped out of working with our ego and are using part of our astrality instead. Another indicator of the presence of warmth in our ego is humor. Steiner says that humor is a hallmark of real spirituality.

No other sense is so filled with emotions as our sense of warmth. Anger is part of this. We can heat up and go red in the face with anger or we can go cold and white with rage. Anger can run amok when our ego is not in charge of it, but when our ego is using anger in the right way it becomes a true educator for our higher self. It can become the corrector of our unconscious. It wakes us up. When we meet injustice with righteous anger we form the will to correct it. In this way the sense of warmth gives us the possibility to evolve. If we could never feel anger we would also never be able to feel love.

If the world was only made of light and did not contain warmth there would be no time. We put something in the freezer to slow down time. The words temperature and tempo are connected.

When children have not yet developed a right relationship to this sense they may have a more difficult time identifying their feelings. They might need to work hard to identify things like fear, anger, or sadness. They may be able to feel these things, but not be able to put them into words. When the child's sense of touch isn't working in the way it should the child will have difficulty forming memories. When this is combined with a difficulty with the sense of warmth the child will sometimes feel overwhelmed with emotion. Without the sense of touch to mediate and provide the ability to form cohesive memories, the child's disembodied feelings will feel like a tornado. The child will feel them surrounding him or her, but those feelings will never land long enough for him or her to identify them and put them in context. They may have the feelings but lack the context to work them through. This could cause them to form false conclusions about the causes of their feelings. They may have strong emotional reactions to situations that don't really exist, and so are all the more difficult to resolve. When their sense of soul or emotional balance is not present to help them find the middle ground they will be truly lost, vacillating between extremes and unable to find the reality of the middle ground.

When a child is struggling with the sense of warmth they may not form a right relationship to anger so that instead of being able to hone their anger and use it as tool, a catalyst for making changes, it could become a bludgeon used to bully others. It also could become something they turn inwards against themselves. Unexpressed anger becomes depression, a feeling of hopelessness.

Sense of Hearing

The sense of hearing is the first of the highest senses. Through hearing the threshold of the spiritual world approaches us. The spiral of the stars in the cosmos is echoed in the spiral of our inner ear. The spiral is the form that enables the spiritual to form out of the material. This is what transpires when we truly hear. What might have remained merely noise becomes music or the voices of nature and human beings. An artist is always a listener. The sense of hearing and the sense of balance have the same beginnings in embryology, but because balance orients us to the earth and hearing lifts us up to the spiritual they become polar opposites.

When we can move fluidly between balance and hearing we are *listening*. We can only truly listen when we have found inner balance. We listen out of that place of stillness within ourselves. Listening arises out of the social element. We have to want to connect. At present we need the help of our angels to completely listen to each other. We are still too egotistical to do this without their help. It will only become possible to listen without the help of the angels when we have developed a true social life, when we have love in the social realm. For now, the angels carry us in this work. For every community that is formed, for every relationship between two people, the help and protection of the angels is necessary.

Our own sense of hearing existed before we did. We formed

ourselves by listening to the music of the spheres. Our ear is shaped like an egg, a symbol of the mother. It signifies our own creative impulses.

When we take in sound as noise we use our physical body. When we can differentiate beat and harmony we are using our etheric body. To recognize the sound of a human voice we need to use our astral body. When we can rise up to the realm of pure tones we will be using our spirit.

When a child is in a thin-skinned condition, not really in his or her body, he or she will hear as if they are at the end of a long tunnel. Sometimes things may seem so far away to this child they will not feel the need to respond to what they hear. Extraneous noise can be painful to this child. They will complain about noise at home or at school and will be really grateful when there is quiet in their environment.

This may be a child who speaks very softly and slurs their words. Their speech may be heavy in undifferentiated vowel sounds. They may prefer not to speak at all, preferring that you read their mind.

With the child in the thick-skinned condition you might notice that they speak with an exaggeratedly loud voice. They have not yet learned the relationship between distance and volume, so they may talk to the person next to them just as loudly as they would the person across the room. To speak loudly is also a form of pushing, which is the universal gesture for this condition. This pushing quality may cause them to trip over their words in the form of stuttering. If the kind of acquisitiveness that Steiner talks about begins to form, the one that can lead to kleptomania, the child may start "collecting" sounds and repeating them endlessly. They may punctuate their interchanges with groundless screaming.

This child's speech may have a mechanical or metallic quality. They may habitually mispronounce certain consonants, remaining stuck in the way they began speaking them as toddlers. If you notice that a child has a difficult time with certain consonants, but can pronounce them quite clearly when they find them in a new word, or are speaking them in a poem that is new to them, this could indicate that the child doesn't have a "speech" problem per se, but more of a thick-skinned "stuck" problem,

This child may have a very difficult time with music. They will not be aware of the subtleties of rhythm or beat, and will not be aware of the other enough to feel compelled to join in or match the rhythm of the group or follow the tune the others are singing. Because music is movement, and movement is challenging for them, they may have a hard time following a melody. They may sing off-key, or only be able to sing one or two notes, which they will repeat over and over. They may feel that music is a race, and whoever finishes first wins.

They will have a very difficult time listening, because they have yet to find the balance between the need to express their own thoughts and the needs of others to express theirs. In class you will notice that they always know exactly what you are going to say, and may begin to do it themselves before you get to the end of your presentation or instructions. Actually, they will think they always know, but most often they will be wrong.

Sense of the Word

This is the sense that allows us to recognize something as human language. In the human voice all the elements of musical instruments are combined. This is the sense of communication or contact. In order to access this sense, one must first have a consciousness of self. Through the sense of the word we realize that a word is a word, and not just some arbitrary conglomeration of sounds. When we have no language in common we use the language of gesture to illustrate our intent. The movement of gesture has meaning. This is the sense of the word made visible. To understand that words and gestures have meaning, to understand the languages of nature or architecture requires not just a taking in of what is around us, but a comprehension of what is around us.

Words are made up of consonants and vowels. The consonants are the bones of language and the vowels are its soul life. These things are the instruments of God. There are archangels standing behind languages. When you listen to a language you are really listening to the being of an archangel. Steiner tell us that when we begin to understand something about this connection we will begin to understand something about our Spirit Self.

When the sense of balance is not in order, the labyrinth or the inner ear will not be able to take in sounds in a meaningful way. This means that when the sense of balance is not in order the child will have a difficult time developing the sense of the meaning of the word. The sounds may not organize themselves into meaningful words; they might remain as just random noise. This could make it very difficult for the child to form speech correctly and it could also make reading much more of a challenge. In order to connect the symbols of our alphabet that make up words into something meaningful you first have to hear the sounds, and let them resonate in the quiet of the inner ear where we experience balance. You must hear the word in your head before you can read it.

This is another reason, besides difficulties with the sense of their own movement, why following instructions may overwhelm the child. Prepositions may really be confusing for the child. They may not be able to form a correct inner picture for words like "by" or "at" or "near" or "under." This can be reflected in their difficulty understanding gesture or social cues. You may notice they interchange certain words that seem similar to them, words like "that" or "what." Following directions can be much easier for this child is we only give them one or two things to listen to at once, and punctuate our words with illustrative gestures.

When the child is in a thick-skinned condition they may not be able to tell the difference between a monologue and a dialogue. They may speak right over someone else. If two or more children who are in a thick-skinned moment are seated together they may have dueling monologues and never notice that no one else is listening. They can be very literal, and will not get the point of humor. They may feel it to be some kind of trap and react with anger.

When the child is in a thin-skinned condition they may not have enough of a sense of touch combined with a lack of the sense of the word to reach out towards the other to touch them with their hearing. This may mean they no longer have a desire to understand the words of others. They may allow all sound to become noise, and not differentiate between music, the sounds of nature, or other people speaking to them. They may shut all this out, push it away, and work to remain separate within the bubble they create for themselves. Although they may hear these things just fine, they will have lost their desire to respond.

Sense of Thought

The sense of thought is the ability to understand meaning. This is the realm of pure ideas, the archetypes, which cannot be expressed in words. These are the things that live on a plane higher than language. Creation is beyond language. Understanding and truth are beyond language.

Truth is something we can never comprehend until we can comprehend dichotomy. We have to balance something dichotomous within ourselves to come to truth. We have to struggle with it. A child who is never allowed to experience the pain of struggle will never develop a feeling for truth. This is why it is so important to let the children struggle to answer their own questions. Our job is to educate. The word "educate" comes from the Latin meaning to draw out. Our job is to ask the right questions that will lead the child towards drawing the truth out of themselves. We have to accept completely the picture Steiner gives us of the milk jug. In Lecture Two of *Curative Education* Steiner tells us,

> All investigations which set out to discover where thoughts could originate in man are, in the eyes of Spiritual Science, no more sensible than if someone who had a jug of milk given to him every morning were to begin to ponder, in his cleverness, how the china of which the jug is made produces the milk. It might conceivably happen that he had never observed how the milk does get into the jug. But if he were to start wondering how the milk manages to ooze out of the china, we should take him for a simpleton indeed. To assume such a possibility in regard to a milk jug is obviously to adopt a hypothesis which leads to an absurdity. And yet, in regard to thinking, science makes this very hypothesis; science is just as stupid, every bit as stupid as the fellow we have imagined. For when we set out to investigate with all the means afforded by Spiritual Science we find nothing at all in the human organization that could possibly produce thoughts. There is simply nothing there capable of doing it. Just as the milk must be poured into the jug in order to be in the jug, so for thoughts

to be in a human being, they must *come into* the human being. And whence do they come—for the life we are considering, between birth and death? Where are thoughts?

Steiner tells us the thoughts are given to us before birth. They are a gift from the spiritual world. Archetypical thoughts are the milk we are born with. Our jug is always full, it is just a matter of finding a way for it to flow, and sometimes that will involve struggle or suffering. Our "milk" may have been poured into a physical body, a jug that makes it more difficult for the milk to flow out. The child may have to struggle to reform his or her jug into a vessel that makes it easier for the milk to flow out, but this struggle is the raw material of wisdom. Wisdom is the crystallization of struggle and suffering. We could never follow the thoughts and feelings of others and understand them with compassion without the presence of our own suffering to awaken that compassion. This is the fruit of an awakened sense of life. To practice this transformation of suffering is to form the capacity in human beings to connect to one another and then to be able to connect all of creation together.

This is the one sense that cannot be altered because of the conditions of the polarities. The archetypal ideas are always there. The milk is there. The child may still be striving to have the ability to express them fully, but that does not mean there is nothing there. Steiner says there are really no children with a lack of intellect. What may be lacking is the will to express it. In all children, no matter how extreme their difficulties may seem, you will have moments where you see great insights flash up in them. They will have moments of incredible self-awareness and compassionate understanding. These are just the forerunners of all they will have to express when we have helped them to help themselves to heal their own milk jugs.

Sense of the I of the Other

This is the ability to know that the "other" is also an entity, that he or she is also an individual. This is the sense that allows us to not only hear what the other is saying, but also to understand the meaning that is specific to that particular individual. This is what educates us as to who it really is behind the words and ideas. It is what allows us to feel the sincerity of what the other is say-ing. Through this sense we can also begin to become aware of the elemental beings, the creative or destructive forces that lie behind the other's words. This is something we can even begin to hear in another person's voice when we hear it over the phone.

In order to read the other we must be strongly present in our own being. This is the fruition of our sense of touch. This is where it all comes full circle. A newborn comes into the world with a complete sense of the I of the other. This is why we like looking at babies so much. In their eyes we see our highest selves reflected back to us with complete acceptance. If we want to maintain this ability as we age we have to work to stay firmly centered and at home in our bodies. In order to greet the other we first have to have made a castle out of our own body. When we are rooted in our own skins we can then send our "knight" out from our castle to greet the world. Everything we do to build up our sense of touch is work that will also build up our sense of the I of the other. The more we know ourselves the more we are able to see through the masks and walls others create for themselves and begin to see them clearly right through to the essential being. To truly see the I of the other involves much more than just perceiving their physical presence. To see the I means to see the eternal component which is beyond race, tribe, folk, or culture. The I does not have an age or sex. When you see this in someone it is impossible not to know that they are equally as valuable and important as you are.

When this sense is not fully present the child will respond as if they are alone in a room full of others. The child in a thick-skinned condition will endlessly interrupt or push someone out of their way when they need something. They may feel justified in causing the other pain or distress because to them the other was merely an obstacle in their way. They would push a chair out of their way too. They will not be able to understand what is wrong with pushing a person. They will lack remorse. Murder would be the ultimate immoral act of a person without the sense of the I of the other.

The child in a thin-skinned condition will overly identify with others. They may become hypervigilant, feeling compelled to keep track of the movements of everyone around them. Without the grounding in their own sense of self-awareness, in other words, the sense of touch, these perceptions can become a paranoid web of fantastical imaginiations. They will lose their trust in others, imagining an enemy behind every pair of eyes.

*

In his lectures on the seven life processes, König speaks of the process of secretion as one of transformation and metamorphosis. What has been given to us has to be taken hold of and changed. The pictures of the polarities have been given to us, but it is up to each person to take hold of them in one's own individual way; I have to be able to metamorphose those pictures into something I can begin to work with myself. We all take in the experiences of the senses in a way that is very personal, and as we go through the pictures of the potentials and possible shadow effects of the senses, we can feel how each of us has experienced the world being illuminated for us through the senses, and ways in which our world has been darker, when we have struggled in our development of the senses. This is why we can use them as a latticework upon which we can grow our compassion for the other. When we meet the other and bring our own "secreting" to that meeting we begin to build an understanding that will lead us to some truly practical "digesting" of our experiences. Our transformation into curative educators and curative parents has begun.

Secretion is connected to our sense of taste. We will begin to taste the ideas that come towards us as we take them in and try to digest them, and we will develop an ability to sense when this food tastes good or bad. Just like the food we eat, we can chose to let the difficulties the children we are working with be tasted, welcomed into our own experience, or we can keep those experiences outside of ourselves, where it will remain distant and mysterious.

Drawing from Steiner's work, König also connects "secreting" to "sound." Just as food remains merely texture without taste, so does sound remain noise when we don't learn to use our etheric body, astral and ego to be able to differentiate noise into beat, melody, the sounds of nature, and the sound of the human voice. We have so many experiences of things we observe in the children that would remain merely "noise" if we didn't begin to allow all of ourselves to approach those observations with our own sense experiences. Just as Steiner speaks of the will remaining "instinct" if we don't deepen it through the strength of our ego, so too does he say that "secreting" can remain instinctual, never evolving through "drive", "desire," or "motive." We have to use the potential for understanding in each of our four bodies if we want to evolve the potential for "secreting" to become a tool for healing.

There is one more very practical way we can use our own experience of "secreting" for better understanding the children. We can do what Steiner did when he wanted to better understand the children who were brought to him: watch the child walk or run. We watch them out of pure observation. We don't form any conclusions, or have any checklist in our minds that would muddy the "taste" of the experience. We watch the child move, and then we memorize that movement so thoroughly that we are able to replicate it later on when we are alone. When we are alone we move as the child moves; living into the child's experience by living into their movement. Our body will tell us what we need to know. As we move like the child our body will experience what the child experiences. Then we have to ask ourselves what we would do for ourselves if we felt that way. The things that have helped us move through our own difficulties will be a big clue toward understanding what will help the child.

As we move we can ask ourselves: What is this child's relationship to gravity or to levity? Is this child too contracted or too much in expansion? How is this child's balance? What is their relationship to right/left, above/below, and forward/backward? Are these three planes of space working in sync? Steiner says that the right/left plane is related to thinking, the above/below plane is related to feeling and the forward/backward plane is related to the will. We can tell much about the condition of the child's soul forces by watching them walk and run and then living into their movements. It can tell us a lot about how the child is doing academically, socially, and emotionally. What do we experience that tells us about the child's relationship to his or her senses, particularly the four lower ones? In this way we can begin to intuit our way into the child, using the pictures of the polarities as a framework, and begin to come to some real understandings. If we live with these understandings quietly, again, not jumping to superficial conclusions, the ideas of what to do will begin to transform themselves from vague inklings to moments of inspired will. Then we only need the courage to act.

5. MAINTAINING

Before any significant progress, before we take any meaningful steps forward there is always a pause. There is a moment when we come to a stop, and pull ourselves in. It is the moment of stillness before the diver takes the great jump, or the painter picks up the brush to make that first stroke. It is the in-breath we hold for just a moment, before we step towards the new endeavor. This moment doesn't last long, and we have to be paying attention or we miss it. It is an experience of ego, of the reality of our inner space, a place of preparation. Steiner has given us the possibility of experiencing these moments in structured and rhythmical moments during our day. These are the times we take for meditation. The meditations he gives in *The Curative Education Course* are unique and specialized. They are also succinct and practical. When we begin to work with them we notice that they are like a little in-breath, they prepare us to take our first steps into growing, into becoming curative educators who are able to work independently.

One of the first meditations Steiner gives in the Curative Course is this:

> I am doing something which generally the Gods do in the life between death and a new birth. (Lecture Two)

He says that the fact we know this is of untold significance, and that to be able to think it is most important. He tells us to bring this thought before us every day, as a meditation, as one says a prayer every day, and that this will endow our astral body with the character and tone it needs.

Rudolf Steiner describes a time between death and a new birth when we are spirits among spirits. We enter into the spiritual world and are surrounded by spirit bodies of other human beings in their cosmic immensity, splendor, and completeness. We are surrounded by the splendor that created us. We see this perfection around us, recognize, in it, what we need to become, and thus begin to weave a garment for ourselves, the garment of our future body, for our next incarnation. The spiritual "weavers" help us to do this; help us to locate the various threads we need to build up all of our various forms. And not only the spiritual beings help us in this work, but also all of the human beings who are connected to us. This body will be as big as the entire cosmos, and it will be perfect. As we begin to descend into a new life, we start with this perfection, but then we have to pick up the bundle of karma from our previous life. This karma may not allow us to form our new physical body in the ways it was meant to be. Thinking back to the image of the milk jug, this would be a reason why our jug does not let the milk flow as it was meant to. We still gather the thoughts (the milk) in all their perfection, but we may find ourselves in a body that makes it difficult for that milk to flow.

When we are working with children we see that they come in many variations of milk jugs. Some are very efficient; others not so much. What we may not do is to say that it is the karma of this child to be in this kind of jug and so we need to leave it at that. Steiner is clear in *The Curative Education Course* that it is our job to change karma. The meditation, "I am doing something that generally the Gods do in the life between death and a new birth," is our catalyst to begin to imagine those changes in karma.

Every night, before we go to sleep, we meditate on the children. We hold a picture of the child before us as the child is in his or her highest self. This picture is the template for the "weaving" we will do, as we try to bring the child what he or she needs to complete their milk jug. This is the meditation we need to help us wake up each day with some idea of what "threads" we need to bring each child in our work as "weavers," in order to help them to heal, to become their highest selves.

In the first of König's lectures on the seven life processes, he speaks about his experiences with Ita Wegman. He describes her as a healer, saying:

> Without doubt she was the greatest doctor, physician, that I have ever met. Do not think she was clever: she was wise, but not clever. In one way or another she used everything in order to heal; a remedy, a massage, a strong word, a loving

look, a piece of music, a painting, a walk in the countryside; whatever was available she took and used. She was not like some doctors who just used a remedy and perhaps an ointment but nothing else, because for them medicine has become so narrow. They have forgotten that the whole world, if taken in the right way, is therapeutic. She recognized the same spirit of brotherhood in everything that was alive, that was ensouled, that was inspirited, and she used it all to heal.

This is what we have to learn to do. As we work with the children in our care we have to find just the right moment, look, story, task, or thing of beauty; it could be anything, and we have to know just the right time to apply this medicine. This is not something we will come to all on our own, but, working with this meditation, we will begin to notice that the right ideas are brought to us. We only have to have the courage to use them. They are the "threads" we will use to help the child weave him- or herself into the image of their own highest self. This is the work of the Gods between death and a new birth.

This brings us to the next meditation. "I can do it." This is perhaps the most direct and practical meditation from Steiner that there is. Four simple words: "I," as in *me*, the person inhabiting this body (and not anybody else!); "can," as in *am able to*; "do," as in *engage your will and get busy*; "it," a purposefully vague word referring to *anything needed in any situation*. Steiner says "we need to tell ourselves this with courage and with energy, not just at some particular moment, but carrying it constantly in our consciousness, without vanity, in a spirit of self-sacrifice, and in earnest endeavor to overcome all the things that hinder." This little meditation is a real gift. It is a message of encouragement coming to us directly from Steiner. You can feel the friendliness of his intentions to get us moving and working on our own. It is something we can "pull out of our pocket" any time we need it. Whenever we feel discouraged it can give us the courage to keep moving forward, one step at a time.

Next is a pair of meditations for framing the day. The first is for the evening and consists of the thought, "In me is God." He says we can think of this as the spirit of God or whatever expression we prefer, so long as it's not theoretical. In the morning we meditate on the thought, "I am in God." Steiner says to let this shine over our whole day.

In the evening, we breathe out with our astral body and ego into the cosmos. We become as big as the entire cosmos, and God is contained within us. In the morning, as we contract and breathe back into our physical and etheric body, God becomes our container. Just as we are striving to be the container for the children we work with, there is something bigger than us, holding us. This image can help us to feel we are not as alone as we think we are. Steiner says we then have to realize that both these meditations are one and the same.

He illustrates this further by giving us this pictorial meditation; he says, "Imagine a point within a circle. Imagine a circle containing a point. In meditation let the point become the circle. Let the circle become the point." One of the things we have to develop in order to become Curative Educators is what Steiner calls "etheric" thinking. This is the thinking we do with our heart, not our head. This is the thinking of thoughts that are archetypical, that are created out of the cosmic ether, the thoughts that fill our milk jug. This is the kind of thinking one can acquire by reading (and thinking) Steiner's *Philosophy of Freedom*. Etheric thinking allows us to hold two diametrically opposed thoughts as true simultaneously, the thinking that is at home with dichotomy. This is the kind of thinking that will allow us to see the child in front of us who is struggling and, simultaneously, see the genius in that child. This is what gives us the inner flexibility to see both things as equally true.

At the very end of the Curative Course (in Lecture Twelve), Steiner asks:

> What does it mean when we value our own I too highly? [...]The I that we have now is in process of becoming; not until our next incarnation will it be a reality. The I is no more than a baby. And if we are able to see *through* what shows on the surface, then, when we look at someone who is sailing through life on the sea of his own egoism, we shall have before us the imagination of a fond foster-mother or nurse, whose heart is filled with rapturous devotion to the baby in her arms. In *her* case the rapture is justified, for the child in

her arms is other than herself; but we have a spectacle merely of egoism when we behold someone fondling so tenderly the baby in him. [...] And now, if the teacher will constantly compare this picture with his own daily actions and conduct, once more she will be provided with a most fruitful theme for meditation. And she will find that she is guided into the state I described as swimming in a surging sea of spirit.

He also tells us to meditate on the Spirit Self, saying:

It is really so: the moment we begin to speak of education, we have immediately to make our appeal to spirits who have evolved the Spirit Self. And whenever we try to elucidate what lies hidden in speech, we are actually describing the Spirit Self. I would therefore recommend anyone who is setting out to educate abnormal children, to meditate upon what she can read in our books, about the Spirit Self She will find this a good material for meditation. It is a prayer to those spiritual beings who are of the same kind as the Genius of Language. Such spiritual beings are verily present among us. Say, we come into the schoolroom. If our behavior and gestures as we enter give adequate expression to what we are feeling and experiencing in our soul, then they have an immense influence upon the child. And they are moreover a proof that we are connected with the spiritual beings who bear within them the Spirit Self. (Lecture Nine)

Both of these reflections lead us back to the pedagogical law, and the need to be constantly taking our own inventory, looking to see that we are at our best, not for our own glory, but in order to be of better service to others.

Steiner tells us we must never say, "In order to perceive such things, I should have to be clairvoyant. To say that betokens an inner laziness, a quality that must on no account be found in one who undertakes the task of education." When we take up the work of Waldorf Educators we are told to begin an inner life. Many of us have had the experience of finding that, with time, we can truly trust the fruit of that inner life to guide us in our classrooms. Our prep time becomes streamlined, because something comes from outside ourselves to help us. The right ideas appear. The same thing happens when we begin to work with the meditations in the curative work. We find that the right ideas will come to us in this arena as well. What seems so daunting becomes doable. We are getting ready to grow.

There is a good reason why "maintaining" is placed between "secreting" and "growing." With "secreting" we are moving with our own understanding into the experiences of the child we are trying to heal. This is good only up to a point. If something didn't move in to stop us, then eventually the good we do when we try with compassion to understand would be destroyed. We would "secrete" until we dissolved and destroyed; we would lose the boundary between ourselves and the child we are trying to understand until we melded so completely that we would be lost in our own inner speculations. These speculations would be so permeated with our own egotistical natures—remember that fond foster mother or nurse—that they would no longer be correct. Something has to put on the brakes. Something has to stop us and get us to take a step back and let the higher beings lend us their wisdom. This is the purpose of "maintaining." We have to permeate our experience with Ego so that it doesn't disintegrate into egoism.

König connects "maintaining" with our sense of smell. Remember that the organ for smell, our olfactory gland is located where our third eye is. The third eye is the spiritualization of the olfactory gland. When we work to transform smell from out of instinct it begins to rise into the realm of intuition. It becomes our two-petaled lotus, the organ for discretion. This is what we are honing though our meditations. As we move towards "growing," and begin to try to understand how to work independently with what Steiner presents in the Curative Course, we have to make sure we have the ability to discriminate. When we act on our own we have to first be able to "smell" if our ideas stink or not. We have to work to destroy our egotistical thinking and replace it with "etheric" thinking. In this way we build up our connection with the life ether, the cosmic thoughts that formed us.

In "secreting," we break down though our compassionate understanding the experience of the child so that we can take them in. We begin to "individualize" the experience; but in the world of our will we are still working out of instinct. In "maintaining," we move up in our will out of instinct and into drive, the next stage in will development. With "drive" we are able to build up the inner experiences and understanding of the child in preparation to do something with them.

Meditation is an ego building experience. When we permeate what we take in with ego we transform it into something that can become part of us. König tells us that "Out of the substance which has been maintained, renewed, changed, and metamorphosed, growth can begin from within." It's our own inner work that makes this possible. When we have held what we know in inner stillness long enough, when we have permeated it with our ego long enough, we are then ready to grow.

6. GROWING

This is the place in our development where we need to begin to use will. Our own will. We have to begin to do things out of our own volition. We can't merely copy what Steiner may have done, but he does give us many ideas in *Curative Education* that we can use as a foundation for building up our own work. In order to grow we have to act. In talking about the seven life processes, König connects growing with balance. When we are in balance we have formed a right relationship to space. We can move fluidly within the expressions of the three planes of movement—right and left, up and down, and forward and backward. Steiner connects the right and left plane with thinking, the up and down plane with feeling and the forward and backward plane with our will. When we are ready to grow we are ready to move into action in our thinking, feeling, and will.

Growing means that we leave behind the familiar and move into the unknown. In order to meet the changing needs of the children in front of us we have to be willing to change what we do with them. We can no longer repeat what has been done before. The old prototype is no longer relevant. To grow, we have to begin to take up ideas that are new. Steiner recommends many things for us to take up and make our own in *Curative Education*, but very likely these recommendations are unfamiliar because they were not presented to us in our Waldorf Teacher Trainings. Many of the roots of these ideas can be found in Steiner's autobiography, *The Course of My Life*. Experiences he had as a child, as a youth, and as a young man ripened into the mature insights of the Curative Course.

In the first chapter of his autobiography Steiner talks about his childhood. He describes his interest in the outer world and the long walks he took each day. Walking is a simple thing. It is something that used to be part of everyone's daily life, but few of us today have a real reason to take walks of any significant length on a daily basis.

Instead we drive. In certain places and individual cases this may not be so, but the United States as a whole is an automobile culture. The most basic and simple thing we can bring to the children we are working with in order to help them begin to heal is to provide opportunities for walking and running each and every day. It sounds much too prosaic, but once we begin to really look into the significance of walking it can become the key that opens the door to everything else we need to know.

In *Curative Education*, Steiner says, "When we walk we place ourselves with our ego organization, right into the actual gravity of the earth." What is the significance of that? Think back to the chapter describing the polarities. When Steiner is building up the background for his pictures of the polarities he starts by describing what it means to wake up. When we wake up we should be able to access our senses and engage them in making a connection to the world around us. We should be able to connect to the elements that make up our world: gravity (*earth*), levity (*water*), and breathing (*air* and *warmth*). When we think about the thick-skinned and the thin-skinned polarities we remember that here we have conditions that preclude the child being unable to make a right connection with gravity. This is synonymous with making a connection to the earth. When a child cannot make a connection to gravity it means that all the things that follow are also going to be difficult. They will struggle to connect to the world around them. If they have too much gravity or too much levity they will have difficulties with balance. This will be observable physically, but you will also be able to observe how their emotional imbalance results from a lack of true physical balance. So then we go back to that one sentence of Steiner: "When we walk we place ourselves with our ego organization right into the actual gravity of the earth." As teachers or as parents we are working to help children who struggle to successfully wake up each morning. When a child is struggling with the conditions described in the polarities, we have to understand that the first difficulty they have each day starts at the very beginning. They don't wake up in the right way; they don't come to a complete consciousness or the right kind of consciousness. Walking is a reset button. When we give the child the opportunity to start their day with walking and running we give them an activity that will begin to remediate the first major obstacle they have; coming to a right relationship with the world.

Steiner says that when we are observing someone walk we are also observing the condition of his or her astral body. Again, our three soul forces, thinking, feeling, and will are manifested in how we move, and how our three planes of movement work together. To repeat, Steiner tells us that the right/left plane has to do with thinking, the above/below plane has to do with feeling and the forward/backward plane has to do with the will. When Steiner was asked to observe a child, he asked the child to walk. By watching the child walk he could learn all that he needed to about the child. This is a learnable skill. The best way to learn to live into the experience of a child and understand how it is to be that child, is to watch him or her walk and run and then memorize the movement. If we memorize the child's movement and then replicate it ourselves later on when we are not around the child, our body will tell us everything we need to know. We only have to ask ourselves what we are feeling when we move a certain way and we will begin to have a very clear picture of how the world is for that child. We can feel when one of the three planes is not in sync. We can feel when a child is too gravity-bound or has too much levity. We can see where they are constricted and feel how that affects our breathing. When a child's walking and running is not synchronized we can feel how that makes it difficult for them to take in the world, to focus and to be present. We can feel how certain gestures would make us dizzy and even nauseous, if we moved that way constantly. When we take these bodily experiences and use the pictures of the polarities as a framework we are well on our way to understanding. If a teacher has the opportunity to watch his or her class move in this way every morning it can be a real jump start to knowing what sorts of things to do during Main Lesson in order to counterbalance what has been observed.

The kind of walking and running we would want to use to start a child's day is not the same as we would value later on for play or to burn off steam. Instead, this is work we need to encourage the children to do out of their own consciousness. It is individual work.

We ask them to space themselves, because this movement work is not a social experience. This isn't a time for conversation. It's an introspective time where we want the child to begin to become aware of how their limbs are moving. At first the child's movement will be awkward. Nothing will seem in sync; but with time the activity of walking and running will begin to bring symmetry to the movement. The body will begin to educate the soul and the three planes will begin to be more in communication with each other. At this point we can ask the child questions. We can ask them what their arms or legs should be doing if they are really moving beautifully. We can ask them if this is truly their best work. In this way we begin to bring the child self-consciousness. As they begin to become aware of how their limbs are moving in space many other things will follow. They will begin to form a mastery over their own body.

Steiner speaks in his biography of an experience he had as a young man. He had the opportunity to work as a tutor for a young boy. The child was ten years old when Steiner started to work with him, and the child was in a condition where not much was expected of him. He could not read, nor get anywhere with arithmetic. He was considered so "abnormal" that the family had doubts as to his capacity for being educated. Steiner describes his first task with this boy as "finding access to a soul which was in a state resembling sleep and which must gradually be enabled to gain the mastery over the body. I was thoroughly convinced that the boy really had great mental capacities, though they were then hidden. Through the method of instruction that I had to employ, there was laid open to my view the association between the spirit-soul element and the bodily element of the human being." The boy went on to attend medical school and became doctor.

You can feel these experiences flowering in Steiner's much later description of the "milk jug" in the *Curative Course*. When Steiner explains that all children are born with the milk, that the cosmic thoughts they need are already in their possession but that sometimes the shape of the jug can prevent the milk from flowing, he is reiterating this connection between the ease with which the child can move his or her body in space and the ease with which the child will be able to access all the thoughts and intelligence within them. This soul/body connection is the reason he gives such specific ideas about working with movement.

Steiner's remarks about movement begin in lecture three of *Curative Education*. He says there that we should let the children do gymnastics and to work with exercises for gravity and balance. He tells us we should do things that allow the child to place his ego into the force of gravity, and he reiterates this concept of the importance of the work coming from the child's ego over and over throughout the course. When we really think of the implications of this we realize that what he is telling us will differentiate our work from that of other forms of movement work. Steiner is very clear that we should only be doing work with the children that allows them to work out of their own ego, in other words, their own will forces. This means that movement activities where the equipment or the practitioner are the driving force are not part of Steiner's intentions for curative education. The child must find the way out of his or her own forces. This might mean that he or she will start with the smallest of baby steps. It doesn't matter. It only matters that what they do is done out of their own ego. The connection between balance and the vestibular system is widely recognized, and so activities have been designed to stimulate the vestibular system; but the activities that will have the most profound effect are ones that require the child be 100% present and responsible for their own movement.

The most efficient way to work with balance is on a balance beam, but the beam must be used correctly. According to Steiner, it is in our legs that we experience physical balance; in our arms and chest area we experience soul balance; and in our head we experience spiritual balance. When a child is using a balance beam in the right way all three aspects of balance will be addressed. As balance is connected to speech, correct work in balance will begin to correct the speech difficulties from the roots of the difficulty out. Because a child's emotional balance is reflected in their physical balance when you begin to give them this work on a regular basis you will see that they begin to center themselves and have fewer and fewer emotional outbursts.

The child should move across the balance beam very slowly. Many children can move quickly, but often this can be a compensation for a lack of true balance. You can observe how things really are for the child in balance when you require them to move very slowly, stepping heel-to-toe (physical balance); their arms should be straight to the sides (emotional balance); and their heads should be up as well, not looking at their feet, but focused straight ahead (spiritual balance).

It will not help the child if we demonstrate this for them. We need to give them a picture, an image that they can live into. Sometimes if the child is really struggling it helps to stand on the opposite end of the balance beam, facing them and holding your arms up, just as you want the child to do. Tell them to look right at you, and come straight to you. They will feel that you are holding them etherically and this will make it possible for them to find their own inner balance. There is one other advantage to sometimes doing the work with the children in this way. At that moment when the child is in balance and looking at you, and you are looking into their eyes, you can't help but see them in their highest self. Something really beautiful will come to meet you. The child will know that you see this; they will know that they have been truly seen and this will help them to feel the trust that they need to follow your lead and accept your care.

The first exercise the child can do on the balance beam is to walk slowly across, arms up, head up, and stepping heel-to-toe. When they have mastered this have them do it with their eyes closed. Let them try it going backward, and then backward with their eyes closed. There are many creative variations you can invent that take things even further. When the children have gotten really proficient with balance the next step is to have them do the activities with weights. You can attach the weights to their legs, or have them hold them in their hands. The weight will make them conscious of gravity. In the beginning, the act of coming to balance itself may be challenge enough. Every movement we make requires an inner adjustment to counter the disturbance in equilibrium. When they have found their center with confidence without weights, adding them can give the child an opportunity to find their inner stillness all over again. Because things in life are always shifting and changing it's important that the children learn to find that inner place of balance and stillness over and over, even when the external world is shifting.

If you are working with a child who is struggling with balance to an extreme degree you will need to start with something simpler. Remember, we are always living into the child's inner experience, and, out of that, intuiting what they need, so we have to start at the place we feel they are. For some children that might mean standing on the ground on two feet. You may have to start really simply in this way before adding the arms up and the head looking at you. When they can do this, have them stand on a board placed on the floor, no higher than an inch and as wide as seems comfortable to them. You can also use a rope. When they can stand successfully on the board or the rope try having them slowly walk toward you. If they can't walk slowly (heel-to-toe), continue having them stand. You can count how many seconds they can do this if you want to help them feel their own progress. It may take a year or more to build up to using the balance beam and being able to walk across it. This does not matter! What matters is that they will have been creating true balance for themselves at a pace that allowed the work to come from their own ego. If you "spot" the child on the beam they will never learn to trust their own powers, they will rely on you to do the work for them.

Steiner tells us to get the child to make movements in which he or she is obliged to learn control of his or her external movements: to let them "think themselves" into a stretching movement with the left arm, then the right arm, and then with both arms together; to have them lift one leg, while keeping the other leg still. He says we should get the children to touch their feet with their head, and to let them kiss their toes. Over and over again he tells us we must let the child become aware of the movement of their limbs, their fingers and their toes. In other words, we need to let them develop a sense for their own movement. Again, this is why it is so important that we don't ask them to imitate us, but that we bring them a picture they can live into, so that they can "think themselves" into the movement.

These last sentences are the seeds for a vast amount of creative work on the teacher's part. First, we have to look closely and realize Steiner is asking us to work with expansion and contraction. This is the basic gesture. When we are infants we are born with certain instinctive reflexes. Our limbs flail out in expansion and contract back, but none of this movement comes from the baby's own conscious effort. One of the tasks of the first year of life is to overcome these reflexes by bringing consciousness to expansion and contraction. Often the children we are working with will not yet have completed this developmental step. Out of this understanding we have to get really creative and see how many ways can we bring this basic gesture into meaningful activities for the children. This gives us the opportunity to be continually growing our activities along with the children's growth and progress. When something gets too simple and the child's ego goes to sleep, we then "tweak" the activity to make it challenging again. Just as we wouldn't want to bring the same stale activities day after day in our classrooms, we also want to bring something fresh to the children with their movement work. Think of the equipment you would find in a gym—mats, trampoline, parallel bars, etc.—and imagine how you could bring expansion and contraction using those tools.

The third element we want to bring into our morning movement time is work with gravity and levity. From watching the children walk and run in the morning, it will be clear that some days they will have too much gravity as a group, and some days too much levity. One good way to bring levity into the classroom is by bringing in a small "rebounder" (a type of small trampoline). Even better, bring in two or three and give the children a pattern to carry out. You can work with expansion and contraction on a trampoline as well. If you don't have a trampoline, create some obstacles that they can jump over. Jumping rhythmically brings levity with consciousness.

Having the children do things in pairs as mirror images of each other can bring a kind of gravity. It's a kind of soul gravity, having to do with working with the sense of the I of the other. So can having them move in sync with a partner. This is a good way to begin to develop the sense of the I of the other.

When we watch them move first thing in the morning, as they walk and run we can see what we may need to bring more of later on. Do they need more gravity or more levity? Is today a day to focus more on balance? This means that the movement we include into our mornings is not something that is "set" or routine. We are still Waldorf teachers, which means we are practicing an art. The work we create should be of our own creation. The only litmus test we should apply is to really make sure that the work is calling on the child's own ego and not the teacher's manipulations of the child or the result of equipment that does the work for the child.

All of Steiner's remarks about movement in *Curative Education* have their roots in three main categories: gravity and levity, expansion and contraction, and balance. During the Curative Course, each time Steiner brought in a child who was to be observed, he began by giving a brief biography of that child. In each biography Steiner pointed out important milestones connected to the first years of life that were not completed in a timely way. Something had gotten stuck, most often in the child's first year of life. The tasks of the first year are all related to 1.) the ability to come to a right relationship to gravity, 2.) the ability to expand and contract with consciousness, and 3.) the ability to come into balance. We are born as horizontally oriented, gravity bound creatures. We gradually learn to lift our heads, push up on our arms, roll over, sit up, crawl, and ultimately stand. At first, our arms and legs expand and contract as reflexes. Our own consciousness does not play a part, but we learn to reach out and grasp and bring things back toward us out of our own volition, our own consciousness. When we stand up unaided we have accomplished something huge. We have come to balance! We have overcome gravity. Before we take that first step there is something we have internalized. Of course we can't articulate it, but before we can begin to move in space we have to have a basic understanding of right and left, up and down, and forward and backward. We have achieved an unconscious fluency with the three planes of space. Without exception, the children who are in need of the understanding Steiner provides in *Curative Education* are children who have not successfully completed these tasks. When we watch them move we can observe it. They will remain stuck unless we bring them the right type of movement activities to help them go back to the place where something was not fully achieved, and help them work through those stages. This is working with the "milk jug."

All of these activities are pointed to in Lecture Three, where Steiner discusses the "epileptic" (or, rather, "thick-skinned") child at some length. It's important to keep in mind, however, that all of us are "thick-skinned" or "thin-skinned" at various times. This is why the movement work described in this chapter is relevant to *all* the children we work with.

In addition to the gymnastic-type activities, Steiner also recommends swimming. Water is a wonderful thing! To begin with, it is enough to just have them work with a kickboard and try to get them to move through the water with straight arms and legs. They don't need to start with having their heads in the water. When they can propel themselves fairly well with heads up then it's time to bring in the breathing. It's important that they only turn their heads toward their "worker side." You can gradually build up to the crawl stroke. The butterfly and breaststroke are not so useful for our purposes as they don't support the kind of cross lateral movements that our children need to develop. The pool is also a great place to play with expansion and contraction. It will give the child with too much gravity instant buoyancy.

A side benefit to water is the power it has to help a child work through any emotional upsets or outbursts they may have. Water flows. A child working with water will "flow" though their inner conundrums as well. Most of us don't have a pool handy, but there are always water tasks available in any classroom setting or at home. Filling paint jars, watering house plants, watering outside, doing the dishes or making tea are all "water" activities that can help a child who consistently has meltdowns to become better able to work things through. If you think about a child like Jasper, someone who is prone to outbursts, a recommendation to the parents to have their child swim can go a long way toward improving things at home.

One pragmatic suggestion that Steiner gives for the "thick-skinned" child has to do with the moral difficulties this child might exhibit. He tells us to make up stories for this child, stories where the child's behavior is exaggerated to a ridiculous degree. If the child can see his or her own behavior blown up to comic proportions it can really help them to become aware of this behavior in a way that allows them to access their ego to help them to overcome it. This has to do with the healing power of humor. Humor has to do with warmth; true humor is a sign of ego warmth. If we can get the child to feel the results of their behavior in a humorous way we will have come a long way toward waking up their ego in a manner that will begin to help them to take themselves in hand.

When we want to help the child in a thin-skinned condition we have to remember that what the child is experiencing is fear. They would rather not attempt to do things and to appear not to know. In order to help them to overcome this fear Steiner tells us to learn to do things inwardly with them. He speaks of sitting next to them and doing the thing in tandem, moving our paintbrush or pencil as we would want them to do it, but not literally doing the thing. This can be really helpful if, in addition to thin-skinnedness, the child is also experiencing under activeness. Otherwise, it is often enough to merely be doing the activity inwardly with the child, even from the other side of the room. This requires that we believe the child can do the activity 100%. If the child can feel our certainty, this will empower them to try. We have to see the question behind their fear. They are asking us, "Do you believe I can do it?" We have to answer them with an unequivocal, Yes! If we waver even a little or doubt that they are truly capable we will create an incapacity in the child. Steiner says that everything we think or feel about the child affects them all the way down to their organs. This is a real danger for the thin-skinned child. They have fear. They ask us if this fear is real. They may not ask in words, but they will ask in actions. If we take their fear as a sign they are incapable, and perhaps even go so far as to have them assessed, we will have permanently solidified them in a difficulty that most likely was not intrinsic to their being. They will bring their fear to the assessment, will know they are being judged, and will not be able to show the assessor all of what they really know or are capable of. If we can find it in ourselves to believe in the child, and inwardly follow them to give them courage, we will see over and over again that this child is actually exceedingly capable. Gradually, they will begin to believe in themselves and they will go on with their life without difficulties. We will have circumvented a great pitfall.

Steiner speaks of the benefit of small shocks for the thin-skinned child. By this he doesn't mean anything grandiose or traumatic, just a slight shift in a rhythm or bringing something they don't expect into a normal routine. Even a change in the pace of your lesson can be enough. The purpose of these little shifts is to wake the child up a little. By shaking things up just a bit the child's ego has to wake up too.

As the child begins to heal they will swing back and forth between thick-skinned moments and thin-skinned ones. We will need to learn to accommodate them in all that we do, not only in how this manifests outwardly but in how we hold ourselves inwardly as well. Imagine the eurythmy gestures for "D" and for "B." These gestures can be inner ones as well as outwardly visible ones. They can also be gestures of the voice. When a child is in a thick-skinned moment it helps them if you hold them with an inner gesture of "D," and if you put that gesture into your voice as well. The gesture of "B" will help the thin-skinned child.

For the child with too much iron Steiner recommends something incredibly simple but also incredibly effective. He tells us that when we see that the child has become obsessively repetitive about something we need to whisper. We whisper very softly, "We are done with _____." or "Forget about _____." We whisper because for the iron child our normal tone of voice can sound to them like yelling. If they experience that we have yelled, those words will be the next thing that gets stuck in their consciousness. When we whisper, they can hear us, they can take in our words and they can follow them. When we know that a child has this tendency towards obsessive or repetitive actions we should watch for something that looks like it could be the next thing they may perseverate about and step in fairly quickly. After the third or fourth time we see them stop to retie a shoe that was already tied, we call them over and whisper, "We're done with that now." By being very proactive we can shift them out of the habit of needing to find something new to be stuck on and bring them much further into the present with their thoughts and actions.

For the child with too much sulphur, Steiner recommends bringing them something that they can do or recite at the same time each day. In this way we are helping them to build up a little "island" of recall that they can begin to build upon. Starting with just one thing a day they can be helped to recall more and more of the rest of their lessons. Steiner says that the morning verse is an example of something that is "medicine" for the sulphur child.

When we are working with an underactive child we have to remember that they know what it is we are asking them to do, but they can't get their body to respond. It can sometimes help to give them a little jump-start in the form of a one-word cue. We have to use humor here, and make sure we are giving them plenty of warm eye contact, but sometimes in those moments when you see they are stuck you can help get them moving by giving them just a word like, "Run!" or "Sweep!" or "Write!" If you have done this appropriately they will giggle and then move on.

The overactive child needs to be brought to stillness. This has to become an important piece of every teacher's classroom management and something that every parent learns to use during transitions at home. In the classroom you hear teachers repeating the same instructions over and over again, such as "I need everyone to listen," or "I need everyone to be sitting quietly," or "Get out your Main Lesson Books," or "Line up at the door." Or, even worse, "Shh! Shh! Shh!" We give out group instructions like this every time there is a transition. We say these things, but many of us have become accustomed to being ignored. We have gotten so used to it that we no longer take ourselves seriously. We think if we are muddling through with the children more or less doing what we ask things are OK. We think that chaos is an acceptable state in the classroom all the time. Chaos has its time and its place, but it is not a permanent state. Our lessons need to breathe, and each in-breath, before breathing out, should come in all the way to quiet. Classrooms today contain more and more children who are struggling with an overactive condition, and so each teacher needs to bring in this moment of quiet every time he or she asks the class to transition. Generally, we think we should be satisfied if most of the children are listening to us, but it is precisely the children who tend to ignore us the most who need this moment of stillness the most. When we move on before they have achieved it, they learn they are not important to us and so they will push even harder to disrupt the class so that they can have our attention. They need to feel they can trust us to mean what we say. We have to learn to wait for each child. It takes three weeks to create a new habit. It might mean three weeks of frustration to get there, but if we hold the children to an expectation that they come to stillness before transitions they will create this as a new habit. The classroom will be a much happier place. No one will feel overwhelmed by the constant noise and chaos we have developed calluses in our soul over. Each child will feel seen and appreciated. That one little moment of stillness is incredibly important. It lets the children feel our etheric holding of them. The other element of this holding is to sense when things are about to go too far and bring them in *before* they behave in ways that will earn them a consequence. We need to start setting our children up to succeed.

*

These are the things we can do to work with the conditions of the polarities. We also have to be thinking of ways we can support the four lower senses at home and in the classroom. Starting with the sense of touch—what is it that we really want to support here? To best support the sense of touch we have to think of all the ways we can bring appropriate boundaries to the children. A majority of the children with difficulties will have them because they have not had sufficient or appropriate boundaries at home or at school.

Think of a newborn baby—what would the first boundary look like that we would need to bring to an infant? Many cultures recognize the importance of swaddling the infant and carrying them close. Our great grandparents probably recognized the significance of dressing a child warmly, including head, hands, and feet. This used to just be common sense. How often do we see infants these days dressed as miniature versions of their parents? If the parent feels comfortable in shorts and a sleeveless top, then this must be good for baby too. Of course some days really are hot, and then an infant will indeed need to be dressed lightly, but for the most part an infant needs his or her arms and legs to be covered. He or she needs a hat. This is part of helping them to form a relationship to the organ for their sense of touch, their skin. This is particularly true for an infant that was born cesarean and therefore missed out on that first experience of touch they would have received from passing down the birth canal. It's important that babies are dressed warmly and it's important that the carriers we put them in truly protect them, keep them snugly, and give them the feeling of being contained. Baby carriers, such as slings, that form a cocoon for the baby are great. Carriers that situate the baby facing forward, with arms and legs dangling, and at the mercy of the person wearing the carrier, are a set-up for a child who may struggle to fully develop their own sense of touch later on. Imagine being strapped to the chest of a giant, unable to control your arms and legs. The world is coming at you, and there's nothing you can do about it. If you look at the expression of a baby in such a carrier you will see the "deer in the headlights" look already strongly developed. How is this child to develop trust in the world?

Dressing a child in layers seems so prosaic. We can't quite believe that it is so important. But Steiner emphasizes it quite clearly, speaking of the hardening that can come about later if the child isn't dressed appropriately. He says it's particularly important for the child prone to seizures that they are dressed overly warmly. The seizure is an attempt on the part of the astral and ego, which is stuck too far into the physical-etheric to come into contact with the skin; in other words, to find a healthy balance. Remember that this child is not likely to sweat. If they are dressed overly warmly to the point that they do sweat, this is an indication that the astral-ego has made contact with the skin. This can mean that a seizure is averted.

Clothing provides a physical boundary, but just as important are the soul, spiritual, and emotional boundaries. A child is not meant to be in charge. A child is born needing grownups around him or her that can guide and protect. This is how the child develops their sense of touch, and remember, every other healthy stage of development arises out of a strong sense of touch. A child needs to feel that the grownups are in charge. Then he or she can relax and enjoy being a child. It is not uncommon to hear parents or caregivers ask a very young child their preferences as to what they want to eat, where they want to sit in the restaurant, what they would like to wear, etc. A huge meltdown on the part of the child often follows these discussions. The child rightly feels overwhelmed and vulnerable when decisions like this are asked of them too early. What parents and teachers need to understand is that the child left alone with these types of decisions is a child that feels abandoned and fearful. Eventually this child will be at risk for an incompletely developed sense of touch. This will snowball through the rest of the senses until the difficulties will be reflected all the way into and through the physical body. In this way a child with real difficulties will have been created. This will not be a child who was born into a body that was difficult to incarnate, it will be a child whose biography was such that they were not able to form a correct relationship to their own sense of touch though the organ of their skin. Proper boundaries at home and at school then become the remedy for this child. Autonomy should come gradually and follow the course of true child development.

The foundation for forming a strong sense of life is rhythm. Rhythm is important for all children, but it is especially important for the child who is trying to find his or her way out of the extremes of the conditions of the polarities. When this child can experience consistency in the times they wake up and go to bed, in meal times and in the breathing in and out of their day, they will begin to internalize these structures. This will allow them to begin to truly reside inside their skins and become aware of themselves as human entities. Karl König makes the connection between what is known as "Spectrum Disorders" and the sense of life. When we understand that the sense of life is vulnerable in children who might be given this label, we can understand the importance of doing everything possible to bring rhythm and structure to these children. The more a child begins to live inside his or her own skin, the more present they become, and the more they are then able to know that the body they have been carrying around is really them. A child who feels securely present inside his or her skin is a child who will have a much easier time with transitions. Such a child will be ready and able to move into the world through the gifts of all their senses.

An additional way we can support the sense of life is to make sure the child eats a healthy and varied diet. Many times the children we work with have such a small awareness of their own sense of life that they don't realize they are hungry. This makes them disinclined to eat. Combine this with a lack of the sense of touch and food becomes merely texture. This child isn't yet able to "touch" their food with their sense of taste. The result is often a child who will only eat a handful of foods. This can affect both their speech and their ability to learn to read. Our tongue contains different regions for different types of tastes. When the child is given a variety of tastes at each meal the tongue becomes engaged. This helps it develop the flexibility required for correct speech. In order to learn to read fluidly the child must first be able to hear the sounds that the different letters make as they form them in speech. If the tongue has been allowed to remain sleepy the speech will follow, and possibly the sound recognition as well.

The first step towards developing a child who is a healthy eater is to make sure meals follow a rhythm. The rhythm will help the child to identify the feeling in their belly at mealtime as "hunger." The next step is to encourage that each food on the table be tried. Many children will swear they hate a food they have never tasted. This is why it should not be up to them to decide what they will chose for their meals. Rather than make disgusted noises and loud refusals at the table the child should be given the choice as to whether they would like a regular or a small serving of every dish. It may need to be a very small serving. It is never too early for them to learn to ask politely—saying "Please" and "Thank you" is also a great way to enhance our consciousness of others. All of us end up finding foods that we truly don't care for, and with time it will become clear which foods are truly not palatable for each individual child, but that list should be limited to one or two things.

It's easy to see how working with movement can support the sense of own movement. What we generally overlook, however, is the importance of normal everyday movements. Every time we ask a child to complete a task we are working on the sense of movement. Every time we ask them to sit correctly at the table or at their desk we are working on the sense of movement. The goal is to bring consciousness to movement. That means we are working with the will. When we work with the will, we strengthen the ego. When we strengthen the ego we are building up the capacity within the child to heal him or herself.

Again we can look at Steiner's biography to find the roots of his thinking about movement. He speaks of sitting in a classroom as a young boy and being asked to copy out sections of a book verbatim. He talks about how his hand moved mechanically across the page without engaging his intellect. In other words, his will was not engaged. Over and over in *Curative Education* Steiner finds as many ways as possible to get us to understand the importance of letting the child do things out of their own forces. He tells us to give the child things to do that are not complete, to let them make a mess, to allow them to struggle. He himself became engaged in school when he met teachers that provided him with the opportunity to think for himself. Mindless activities did not propagate his learning.

If we want to support the child's sense of movement we have to eliminate mindless activities from the child's life. One of the most glaring examples we can find of a mindless activity is the habit of having children copy from the board. It might make for more homogeneous Main Lesson Books, and might make things simpler for the teacher, but nothing of the child's will or true creativity is involved in this activity. Copying may have been the accepted mode in public schools at the time Steiner founded the first Waldorf School, but there is nothing in Steiner's lectures to teachers that supports its existence in Waldorf schools today. It has become a habit. If you read Steiner's ideas about the first Waldorf School, his plans for the curriculum, you will find he tells us to let the child write (and then read) their own little essays by the end of first grade. It is the teacher's job to bring stories from the curriculum to the child. It should be the child's job to write those stories in his or her own words and enter them into their Main Lesson Books.

Somewhere this means that all of us must work to find the courage to allow the children to create work that is not perfect. We have to get to a place where process is more important than product. Another way of saying this is that we have to come to a place where our pride is less important than the pride the child feels in his or her own work. We can give the children work to do that is more or less complete, and the final product might be quite beautiful. We might then feel that we are wonderful educators. We are only educators if we have drawn out of the children *their* best selves. This is the true meaning of educate—to draw out. If we put aside our egotism we create a place for the children to create their best. Even if that best is less than what it would have been if they had copied our best, the child will feel a great deal of pride in their work, and that pride will be a catalyst for progress. What is the child's best tomorrow will be more than what it was yesterday. We will have a classroom that will hum like a hive, full of children who are engaged and happy.

We have to understand that anytime we as teachers or parents follow along behind the child and fix things we are taking away a piece of the child's self-esteem. If we take on the responsibility for finishing things we might be building up our own will, but we are crippling the child's will. Parents and teachers can become overly invested in smoothing the child's path, thinking that by making the child's life easier, by removing struggle, they are creating happier children. The opposite is true. Steiner says that in order for a child to learn truth they must struggle. When everything is done for the child they have no reason to feel true pride in their accomplishments. Their self-esteem disintegrates. This is how to create an adolescent who fears the future, one who can't imagine going into an adulthood having to make the necessary choices. This is a depressed young person, headed for a life of self-doubt and anger. If we never learn that it is all right to make mistakes we fear to even try. If we become accustomed to having someone clear our path and clean up after us we will only resent employers and life partners who expect us to carry our load.

So this means that at a young age we have to begin allowing the child to be responsible. The three- or four-year-old can put on their own coat and carry their own lunch basket. The five year old can dress herself. By six the child should have meaningful chores at home, so that they feel they are an important part of the family. And we have to learn to back off and let them figure things out for themselves. We might ask them what they need to do to be ready to go to school, but we don't tell them to get their coat, lunch, and homework. Learning to ask the right questions is a great way to build up the child's sense of movement. Instead of lecturing to the child, we ask them what they should be doing. We ask them to think for themselves. If you think of how many times our frustration with the child is involved with them not doing what they need to do you can begin to see how many times of the day can be made smoother if we stand back and let the child figure it out.

This works in the classroom too. We don't tell the class what they need to do, we ask, and then we wait until they figure it out. This can go a long way towards eliminating problems on the playground. If we know that things have become socially difficult during recess we don't lecture the children about the importance of kindness. When we try to address the emotional life through the intellectual we create cynics. Instead, before we send them out to play we ask them what needs to happen during a game. What do you need to see? We allow the children to tell us what playing kindly looks like. And then we ask them to tell us what we don't want to see. They know. After that you can come to a conclusion together as to what might be the consequences if they are not able to play together well. Here again we are being educators. We are drawing out of the child what they need to do to make something successful. This draws out their higher selves. It helps to build up the right kind of ego forces. This helps to build up morality in the will, where it can take root and truly become part of the child's soul life. All of this is part of the child's sense of movement.

When we are trying to build up the sense of balance we always start with physical balance, but we have to go beyond the physical and address emotional and spiritual balance as well. The first step in doing this is to create a living inner picture of each child at his or her best, a real picture of the higher self. We have to become committed to this image. This image becomes our guide in helping to shape the child. When we hold the child in this place we hold them in emotional balance. We are allowing the child to feel what it's like to be centered. It is the job of parents and educators to help the child in this way until they are ready to do so for themselves.

What does this look like practically? Let's say it's the end of the day. The child comes home and they are tired and most likely hungry. The first things they want to talk about are all the negative things they experienced during the day. All of us need to vent to some degree, but when we allow the venting to go too far we are solidifying the child in an unrealistic negativity. First, we need to make sure the child gets a snack and a little bit of downtime. This can go a long way towards turning negative perceptions around. Then what? Maybe the child is really upset because someone didn't do things they way they wanted at school. One choice a parent might make is to pick up the phone or send an e-mail telling the teacher to fix the problem. If the parent does this they have told the child that they don't think they are capable of solving problems on their own. Instead, we can sit with the child and ask them what they could do to fix things. If we are really wise, we will ask the child what their part in the difficulty might have been. We allow a certain amount of time for this conversation, and then we move things into the present. We allow school life to remain at school and focus on what is happening now. This is a great balancer for all of us. This is how we build up equanimity.

The times of the most emotional growth are the times fraught with the most potential for emotional unbalance. The nine-year change and adolescence are examples of these kinds of milestones. The danger in colluding with the child when the child is feeling fearful or disgruntled is that we are then creating a space where the child may become more and more hysterical. They can get themselves so far out on a limb emotionally that they have no idea how to get themselves back. The remedy here is again to bring them back to the present. Help them to articulate what is really happening in the moment, and let go of anything that they cannot change right now. Because the child is already vulnerable during transitional milestones we could be creating a lifelong propensity toward unbalance if we don't help them find a healthier way. A child who comes home every day and only brings the negative learns that negativity is the way to get attention or love. This is not a lifelong path we want them to go down. We want our children to become strong. We want them to be emotionally balanced. This means we have to take responsibility for what we are creating by staying strong and balanced ourselves. We have to let our children struggle and find their own way, find their own solutions. If we become their perpetual problem solvers we will have become the instigator of real problems later on in life.

When we have come to the place where all of this can be "maintained" within us we have come to the place of growing. We are ready to change old patterns and take up new tools. In the hierarchy of will we have moved to the realm of desire. We have to transform this desire into the will to move forward and not allow it to sink into the wish to collect. We can begin to hoard new ideas, thinking that the more we read and superficially assimilate, the more we know. Remember, Steiner says it is not what you know, but what you are that makes you a Curative Educator. We have to grow into the work, making it our own, not greedily acquire new thoughts to sit within us, making us complacent. We have to allow our new ideas to become ripe, but not allow them to rot. When food is ripe we use it. We cook it or preserve it for later use. When our ideas are ripe we have to put them to use as well. We have to harvest our growth in deeds and continue to plant new seeds for future harvesting. We can never be finished with growing.

7. REGENERATING

In his work on the seven life processes König says that when we are ready for the stage of regenerating we have entered into something connected with our sense of movement. We have movement in the form of actions or deeds, and we are aware, conscious of our intent with those actions. Steiner says regenerating is connected with the realm of time. We can look back and see those who have created before us, and hopefully look ahead and imagine others taking up the work in the future, and now we ourselves are able to create a tangible manifestation of a practical application of Curative Education. We are ready to create our own work as curative educators or curative parents. My work has been to create Mulberry Farm. The roots of Mulberry Farm are to be found in Somerset School, which was located in Colfax, California. Somerset School and Farm was the work of Sunny Baldwin, who, with her husband Charles, worked for many years bringing Curative Education to children and families. I worked with Sunny for four years at Somerset, and that was my foundation training as a curative educator. Hopefully some of you reading this book will be inspired to take up Steiner's work in Curative Education and use it to enrich your homes or classrooms or even to start a program like Somerset School or Mulberry Farm.

When Rudolf Steiner started the first Waldorf School he included what he called *Klein Klassen* in his vision. These were small classes, independent of the large school, but close enough to serve the children who needed them. These "little classes" were meant for the students who needed more than the "big class" could give them. Five years after the inception of the first Waldorf School, Steiner gave the twelve lectures that comprise the Curative Course to a group of enthusiastic young people. Their mandate was to learn what could be done to better serve the children whose needs weren't being served in the large class. Somerset School and

Mulberry Farm are examples of programs that could be thought of as *Klein Klassen*. Both of these programs used or are using the philosophy of Rudolf Steiner's Curative Education as their foundation. There is a great need for more such programs. Ideally, there should be a *Klein Klasse* everywhere there are large Waldorf Schools. There is still much work to take up. Thinking back to the first chapter, the children described there are examples of children who most likely would be better served in a Curative program, children who need a smaller setting, and who need much more specific movement work than is possible to do in a large class setting. These are children who would do well in a program like Somerset or Mulberry. Here is a picture of a day at Mulberry Farm. This is intended as a tangible example of what a program working out of Curative Education could look like.

Mulberry Farm is located in Santa Rosa, CA. It is on a small parcel of land, just under three acres. Santa Rosa has a temperate climate. It is very rarely too hot in the summer. Winters bring rain and we some nights bring a heavy frost. We are close to the ocean and the redwood forests, as well as the rolling hills of the Coastal Range. Our property is long and narrow. We have two horses, as well as a pony and a miniature horse, two pygora goats, five ducks, and three rabbits. We have a vegetable garden and have planted fruit trees and shade trees. Two of the teachers live in the house, which also serves as the dining room for students and a place to gather for crafts and other group projects that are best indoors. There are lots of board games stored in the window seat for rainy day recesses. The kindergarten occupies one of the bedrooms in the house. We have a large, finished building next to the house that serves as our gym. We have two small ten-by-twelve feet buildings where the grades age children do their academic work each day. We have a round pen and an arena for riding instruction and a pool for swimming when it's warm enough. We have built stalls and paddocks for the horses. Some of the children built a house for the goats as their third grade building project. (They have also built a fabulous tree house that even has a sink with running water.) A row of redwood trees shades the house and keeps it cool, in addition to giving us a shady place to do crafts or eat meals outdoors. In front of the house is a circle of hay bales surrounding a mulberry tree. There is one hay bale for each child.

At eight o'clock every morning the teachers gather to meet before the children arrive. In the 2014-2015 school year we had fourteen students and four full-time teachers. Teachers have a Waldorf Teacher Training and have either completed or are in the process of completing a Curative Educator Training. This ratio is important for the work with the children, in order for each one to get the kind of attention and support they need. We talk about the previous day, make plans for individual children so that we can best support them, talk over any pertinent communications from parents, and make sure we are all clear about any changes in the day ahead or things later in the week we need to be aware of. At eight thirty we stand to do a verse.

At 8:35 we begin to welcome the children into school, and we begin promptly at 8:45. Knowing that the proper handling of transitions is imperative for our students to have the best day possible we have worked hard with the parents to make the morning drop-off (and the afternoon pick-up) go as smoothly as possible. We ask that the parents not arrive before 8:35. We ask them to stay in the car with their students until a teacher comes out to greet them. We ask this because we know that, were the children to get out of their cars before we are there to receive them from their parents, the anxiety they may feel about the coming day might result in behavior that would start their day off on the wrong foot. We work hard to set the children up to succeed, so we try to eliminate anything we might know is a set up for them.

The children are dropped off in our front field and walk the short distance into the school area by themselves. It's important that they all can experience this independence at the start of their morning. This helps them to feel confident that they can achieve everything the rest of the day might ask of them. They walk past the row of horse stalls and the goat pen on their way to the circle of hay bales around the mulberry tree. This way they get to greet and be greeted by many of the farm animals each morning.

We call the circle of hay bales the farm circle. Each child has his or her own bale, and we have seated each one next to a person who is not going to react negatively to them. Whenever there is a transition during the day we call them to the farm circle so that they can get ready. When the children come to the farm circle we ask them to just sit quietly for a moment or two. They have mostly all come in cars. (A few parents began riding bikes to school with their children! This was great!) Because they have mostly come in cars they need a moment of quiet to gather themselves. We have many birds on the property and they sing every morning. Although we don't have chickens ourselves, neighbors with chickens surround us so those sounds are also heard everyday. Just listening to the birds and breathing quietly helps the children to arrive peacefully.

When we are all present we call the children one-by-one to line up by the gate to head out to the lap track. Each morning we give thought as to who should be first, and who should line up next to whom. If we know two students are likely to get each other going we do not stand them next to each other. Again, we are setting them up to succeed. Paying attention to these kinds of details is important.

The lap track is next to the horse stalls and surrounds the vegetable garden. On the side across from the horse stalls we have planted a row of maples and poplars so that the children can experience the changing of color in the fall, and the leafing out again in the spring. Every year we plant more daffodil and tulip bulbs so that the children can look forward to seeing them flower. Walking and running past the animals and being able to observe the changes of nature are good ways to open up the sense world to the children each morning. The children run and walk for about twenty minutes. They run two laps and then walk one. The track is about an eighth of a mile circumference. They do this work silently, so that they can really be present in themselves and begin to become aware of their own movement; how their limbs are moving in space. It's always amazing to see how in a very few months just the activity of consciously walking and running can bring so much organization to the child's movement. As this begins to happen you can see this progress reflected in the progress they make with gym movements later in the morning, academic progress later in the day, and progress in social interactions all day long. We have the children walk and run until it seems they have really arrived in their bodies. During this time the teachers have been standing at the side observing. We can tell so much about how the night went and what exactly we have received to work with each day as we watch them walk and run. It gives us an opportunity to live into each days gym work in a creative way as well. Watching the children, it becomes clear when they might need more gravity or levity, or more balance later in the day.

We excuse each child one by one to leave the lap track. How much time they do this work is based on how long it takes them to "arrive." We are really looking for the ego to become more settled in than it may have been when the child first arrived. Remember that "When we walk we are placing our ego right into the gravity of the earth." You can see this connection being made in the quality of the child's gaze. Their movement and breathing will become more harmonious. They become much more present. If someone has not yet done his or her best work, they may run a little more until they have. Everybody leaves on a good note. As they are called they each head into the little shelter where their muck boots are kept. They all have muck boots for farm chores. Each time we are moving the children from one location to another we make sure one of the teachers goes first. Making sure that we always are present wherever the children are is an important part of the safety net we create around them.

When the children have changed into their muck boots each of them gets a drink of water and then they move to farm chores. The children do the real work of the farm. They do whatever needs to be done. They feed animals and muck out stalls and paddocks. Working with the horses is often the most sought after chore on the farm. They can feel the trust we have in them to allow them around the horses. The child must be calm and dependable. They have to be aware of where they are, and where the horse is. You might imagine that shoveling up manure would be unpopular, but it's not. The horses come up to the children and nuzzle them. The children speak quietly with the horses and nuzzle them back. The children get to groom the horses when they have cleaned the stalls and paddocks. A child doesn't need to ever get on a horse to be helped significantly just by being around them and caring for them. Other children care for the goats, ducks, and rabbits. The children who have these assignments feel proud of their jobs too. They gather the duck eggs and groom the rabbits. Some of the children may have watering chores. They all work in the garden—planting, weeding, and harvesting. They learn how to install drip irrigation, and they dig big holes to plant trees. They use hand plows to make furrows. The teachers are around to "hold the space." We do not work with the children during daily chores. We step back, and allow the work to be their work. It's their farm they are caring for. They help each other and teach each other and become like a giant family. They receive the kind of pride that can only come from doing the work themselves. It's very different from being the helper of an adult. Our job is to hold them inwardly so that they can do their very best. We are working inwardly so that the children can work successfully outwardly, but they are the ones that get to shine. Farm chores are a direct experience of the sense of a child's own movement. It's a direct application of knowing where they are in space.

When chore time is over we again call them to the farm circle. We wait for each one to look centered and ready to move on and then we send them to the gym. Again, a teacher always goes first. In the gym they change into their gym shoes (we have a lot of shoes!) and sit quietly, ready to begin. Each year before we begin in the gym we ask them what is important for them to do in the gym. They tell us why it matters that they are quiet and calm. If our attention were to waiver someone could get hurt. The teachers need to focus on the children having their turn on the various equipment. The mood in the gym is very reverent. The respect they have for each other is palpable. They know exactly when someone crosses a new milestone and will cheer and clap warmly for each other. We have three four-by-eight feet gym mats, a trampoline, parallel bars, three balance beams of different heights and widths, and various other assorted equipment. We have weights, beanbags, and wooden and copper rods. On a day when we feel the children need more levity we may set up an obstacle course out of gym blocks and small rebounder trampolines. The children jump on and over, maybe remembering a pattern of different activities such as doing a "starfish" on one rebounder and a "tuck" on the next or jumping up on one gym block, doing a 180-degree turn, and jumping off backward. We get them really moving! A gravity day might call for more rolls on the mats. If they have to do log rolls or egg rolls in tandem it causes them to slow down and really "listen with their eyes" to each other. Using weights on their arms or legs while they are doing balance beam work is another way to bring gravity.

Every day the gym work is different. When a certain exercise or activity gets stale we find a way to "tweak" it so that the correct form of resistance comes back into the work. Without this kind of resistance the ego has nothing to feel itself against. The gym is a toolbox. It is full of things that can be used to work with first year of life activities—gravity and levity, expansion and contraction, and balance—in an endless variation of expression. The children love to come to the gym because what we do there is never allowed to become stale. We take seriously Steiner's mandate to have the children do movements that cause them to become aware of the activities of their limbs. We might ask a child who just finished a series of exercises on the mat if his or her work was better during the first half or the second half. We might ask them to show us what their arms and legs would be doing if they were doing a beautiful "starfish." We might ask a child to repeat an activity and make it better than it was the first time.

Often we will end gym time with a relay race or game. We take the basic elements of developmental movement, but create something lighthearted and fun with them. It's great to get the children really laughing. It's a healthy juxtaposition to the reverent feeling that might begin gym work. The movement work in the gym is the continuation of the integration work that began with walking and running. You can see through the year how the four bodies begin to work in sync with each other. The child develops a relationship to right/left, forward/backward, and up/down. Their movement becomes more conscious and ensouled. It loses the random, jerky, disorganized quality it had before. As their physical movement improves, their ability to use their sense of movement in their academics and social interactions improves as well. We work for forty-five minutes every day in the gym. By then the children have moved for almost two hours. They are ready for their day, and now we head for snack.

Meals are very important. Many of the children come with particular issues about food. They may not recognize food as anything more than a texture and so have very little pleasure in eating. They may eat voraciously, but not taste their food. Mealtimes are an opportunity to help them to better come into their bodies. When the children enter the dining room for snack they are coming into our home. They feel how welcome they are to be with us. If it's cold outside there may be a fire in the wood stove. The table is set with real plates, knives, forks, and spoons. We pay attention to serving food that smells as good as it tastes. Even children who have never appreciated their meals notice the smell of cinnamon or sausage. Because they have worked hard before snack they begin to notice they are hungry. It doesn't take long to make healthy eaters out of all of them. This is a way of working with the sense of touch. Remember we "touch" the world with all of our senses. Beginning to enjoy their food is also the beginning of feeling comfortable in their bodies. The sense of touch is supported, as is the sense of life. How the children sit in their chairs to eat their meals is a real reflection of how they will sit in their desks, so we work on table manners. Meals are also an opportunity to practice having real conversations. We grow some fruits and vegetables on the farm that the children harvest and then get to eat, but we supplement that with produce from a local CSA. Everything is organic. Our snack is like a second breakfast. Our menus are healthy and balanced, but also child friendly. They even love our salads.

We tailor gluten-free or dairy-free meals for the children who truly need them. Some of the children come on special diets they do not in fact need. Gluten-free has become a panacea for many things. What we have observed is that the connection between how we "digest the world" and how we "digest our food" is a real one. If children are fed diets meant to be easily digestible they begin to go to sleep in how they take in the world as well. This has a negative impact on their will. Because working with the will is such an important part of the work we ask families to try to wean their children off of special diets when possible. We see time and again that as soon as the children are back eating a "normal" healthy diet they begin to wake up to the world too, ready to take things on. Steiner is clear that dairy and meat are vital for children who are working with their will, so we include those things in our meals. Another reason to try to avoid a special diet is that it gives the child the feeling that something out of their control is not quite right with them. We have seen children who have been told that their behavior is directly connected to eating the wrong foods. This can have an effect on the child's willingness to take responsibility for his or her own action this way, the special diet has the same effect as a pharmaceutical. We would not accept a child on Ritalin type medicines, because of how those things blanket the ego and make it harder for us to access the ego in the child. The food issues are clearly not nearly as extreme, but to a much smaller degree they create the same type of obstacles. We are working to overcome obstacles, not create life long conditions that need accommodating. The one exception to dietary concerns involves white processed sugar. (Which is now sometimes called evaporated cane juice.) This is something we have seen affect all the children negatively across the board. It causes them to be sluggish, aggressive, argumentative and full of mucus. One of our rules for families is that the children do not have white processed sugar. We use coconut sugar, honey, real maple syrup, and sometimes agave. We do not use them to excess, and we have not found them to have the same effect as white processed sugar on the children. We make cakes, cookies, and ice cream for special occasions, all with "legal" sweeteners. Coconut sugar is our favorite. Each child gets to pick his or her own special treat on his or her birthday. Last year carob whoopee pies were a big hit.

After snack we all go to recess. There are generally at least three teachers outside to supervise the fourteen children. The playground is set up so that we can see into every corner. The children play in our giant sandbox (all fourteen can fit in at once), and they swing and climb on the play structure. They build forts around the base of a eucalyptus tree. They take turns in the pedal go-kart. They shoot hoops and play ping-pong. They practice on pogo sticks. They draw great pictures with big colored chalk. They create things at the woodworking bench. Many of them like to work at recess too. They have built the tree house, but they have also constructed two sets of large, heavy-duty farm gates during recess, because that is what is fun for them. They are doers. Because we form such a consistent container for them our recesses are fairly free of altercations. We know what a problem looks like before it happens, and work to help the child solve it before they do something they would not feel good about later. When we see something that looks like it might not end well, we call the child to us and ask them what we saw. We ask them how they are going to fix it and then we send them back to do what they themselves suggested. This helps the children who have not been so successful on the playground begin to reinvent themselves. They begin to believe that they truly are the good children we know each of them to be. This is also a practical way of helping the children to develop the sense of the "I" of the other.

When we are on the playground we stay put. We do not run about putting out fires. When we stay put we create an atmosphere of calm. This allows the children to really play and have fun, often for the first time in their lives. All the grades play together. The big ones will get involved in activities that are really fun, but normally thought of as being for younger children, all in the name of "helping" the little ones. This keeps their childhood more protected and gives them a chance to mature only when they are ready. If you could be a fly on the wall at one of our recesses you would probably wonder why any of the children you observed were with us. They play kindly together. They take turns. They don't say or do hurtful things, but if they forget, they fix it. It's like observing a very large family of the sort we all wish we came from.

At the end of recess, promptly at 11:30 a.m., we again call the children to the farm circle. Bringing the children to stillness during major transitions is medicine for the overactive condition. It is another way of working with the sense of balance. It gives the children a moment to collect themselves so that moving to a new location doesn't give them a feeling of disorientation. If the children have come to stillness before they move on to the next activity they are much more likely to enter into that activity successfully from the get-go. This is another way of setting them up to succeed.

Now we move to Main Lesson time. The Kindergarten children go to their little room in the house for their "work" of indoor play, painting and other crafts, and story time. Besides hearing stories they might act them out with table puppets or put on costumes and become the characters themselves. This helps them to build up their feeling for the inner continuity of a story. It helps them to become better listeners and writers later on in the grades. The room is cozy and just the right size for a small group of children to play in. In the 2014-2015 school year we had two students in Kindergarten. A small group helps the child who has struggled to connect to others find a way to enter into play and become successful.

The grades children are divided into two groups. Each group has their own small classroom and their own teacher. The classrooms are ten-by-twelve feet spaces. The space is small on purpose because the coziness helps the children to feel held. They don't have to struggle to find the extra equilibrium required to "fill" a big space. This year one classroom has three fourth-graders and four fifth-graders in it. The other classroom has one first-grader, two second-graders, a seventh-grader, and an eighth-grader. Again, the small group is important. More than eight children in each class would be too many. Because the group is small the teacher can help each child individually when needed. Lessons are taught "one room schoolhouse" style. Each grade comes to the teacher for their lessons. When they are not having a lesson they are working quietly on completing yesterday's work or preparing what they have been given for today. If they finish that, they each have chalk and a small blackboard where they can practice a form drawing. When they have the drawing just right they can enter it into their form-drawing book. They may have math practice to work on. There is plenty to keep each child purposefully engaged while the teacher is working with another grade.

Steiner intended the stories and subjects of each year's curriculum to be soul medicine for that particular year of development, so each child receives his or her age appropriate curriculum. The academic goals are custom fitted for each child. Sometimes we receive students who have been held back in Kindergarten with the often erroneous assumption that the extra year would enable the child to overcome their difficulties. Most often it does not. The child has the same difficulties when they do enter first grade, only now they are out of "soul sync" with the curriculum. When we can, we will help the child to integrate into their correct grade, so that they are really being met appropriately.

We never do "copy off the board." Ever. In fact, we don't have a blackboard in our rooms. Each child does his or her best work on his or her own. Every word or picture that goes into their Main Lesson Book is their own creation, completed to the best of their individual abilities. Each child (with the exception of first grade) has a "composition book" in his or her desk. The children hear the stories from their lessons and write them in their composition books in their own words. Some children can write a lot and some cannot. One student's best might be to write one or two words from the story on his or her own. That student can then come to the teacher and tell the teacher what they would like to write in their Main Lesson Book. They integrate the words they wrote on their own into their narrative. The teacher will then take the dictation the child has given and write it for the child in the composition book. In this way the child can write their own words in their Main Lesson Book. Before they write it they read it to the teacher. They know what they are writing, and they are practicing their reading skills as they write. They are strengthening their connections to the sounds letters make. They are learning to spell and to form full sentences. As they put the words into their Main Lesson Book the activity is not mindless, because all the work is their own.

Some students can write pages of work, forming whole essays or stories. They hear the story one day and begin to write it in their composition book. A point is made about the different elements of writing. One element is creative. In this stage the most important thing is writing in a way that is interesting. The children are asked to sound out each word on their own, and not to worry too much about mistakes. The second day we will look at what corrections need to be made. The children will be asked to review what they wrote the day before to see if it is really what they wanted to say. We might review the story together first to make sure they have all the elements clearly in their minds. Then they bring their work to the teacher and together it is corrected. In this way children receive a daily grammar and spelling lesson geared just for them. Working with the children in this way creates excellent writers. They learn to internalize the stories pictorially. It builds up their sense of the word, and of thought.

All the children illustrate their work with images they have imagined. They might make a practice drawing first, and then come to the teacher for help polishing it. This way they get a drawing lesson that also meets them where they are.

Because the children have had so much movement before they come to Main Lesson classroom management is not an issue. The classroom hums with focused activity. The children are ready to be at their desks and ready to do their work. Because they are given work to do that truly meets them where they are they never feel frustrated. They go home every day proud of their work. Because the morning movement work has prepared them inwardly to be ready to do their academics they make rapid progress. It's not unusual for a student to accomplish two or more years of academic work in one year.

After Main Lesson we have lunch and then another recess. The Kindergarten students go home at 1:30. The grades students spend their afternoons doing the kinds of things that they would be doing in a large Waldorf School, only they do them in blocks of about six weeks. This gives them a chance to deepen and strengthen. We do handwork, woodworking, music, and crafts throughout the year. At the end of the year we perform a big play. All the grades children have a part. They end their day with a story. It's a peaceful conclusion to a satisfying day.

At three o'clock the parents are waiting to collect their children in the front field where they dropped them off. The parents wait until the child comes to them, and then they head for home.

Again, we are working on successful transitions. If parents were to turn pick-up time into a social time the children would know they were not fully supervised. Something would happen that would make the ending of the day an unhappy one. We know that our children do not do grey areas well, so parents and teachers work together to make the day's end clear and simple. Everyone can go home happy.

Friday's are our "down day." On Fridays we breathe out. We don't do laps in the morning, nor do we do Main Lesson. We often play kickball in the mornings. Everyone has a great time, and because the teachers are there to supervise we make sure the game goes well. The children learn to play organized games without it being a negative experience. We don't keep score, and each child has a turn being the team captain. Everyone on his or her team has to listen to the captain. Kickball is a great game for helping the children find their feet, remember a sequence, and throw and catch a ball. It's another opportunity for the big ones to help the little ones, and this brings sweetness to the game.

We may save a major job on the farm for Fridays. It might be the day we plant a row of trees or move a load of soil into a new herb garden. We have begun to learn about biodynamic farming and have prepared and sprayed the preparations on the farm. The children have made preps, stirred them, and gone out with small buckets and brushes to cover every inch of the property. On Fridays we all work together, teachers and children.

The children bring their own snack and lunch on Friday and we often eat outside picnic style or we might load up the lunches in a wagon and walk down to a nearby creek. We celebrate birthdays on Fridays and sometimes we spend the day making a seasonal craft like Valentines or Thanksgiving decorations. Fridays give us a chance to really focus on social interactions in a relaxed way. Everyone has worked hard all week, so today we will play.

Each child at Mulberry has a riding lesson once a week. They learn to groom the horse, lead it, longe it, and ride it. By grooming the horse they learn to pay attention to where their body is in relationship to something much larger than they are. They learn that they have to be awake and present. When you lead a horse you have to be in charge of the horse. That means you need to be in charge of yourself first. Longeing requires that the children know how to align themselves with something else, as both of them are moving in space.

Riding a horse is an exercise in balance as well as awareness. The children know that if they are not able to be present they will not be allowed to ride.

During the times that the weather is warm enough, each child swims once a week as well. We are taking up Steiner's suggestion. He recommends having the children swim in a "sensible" manner. To begin with it is enough to have the child work with a kickboard. Gaining control of their limbs so that they can kick with straight legs and straight arms is a good start. From there, we work up to the crawl stroke. We teach the child to turn their head to breathe, turning only towards their "worker" or dominate side. The crawl stroke supports the kind of cross lateral movement we are trying to foster when they walk and run.

Another important part of the work at Mulberry Farm is that of parent mentoring. When children have had difficulties those difficulties have often manifested at home as well as in the classroom. Teachers need to learn to become Curative Educators. Parents need to learn to become Curative Parents. Mentoring offers parents support in learning skills that will defuse the difficult times at home as well as offering new ways of understanding the children. Talking with parents about the conditions of the Curative Polarities gives them new ways of understanding their children. We work together to understand the importance of boundaries and rhythm. When we pass the children on to their parents each afternoon we are sending them home to have an afternoon as full of rhythm and structure as their school day has been. The children come to us for healing. Being the right kind of container for the children is an important part of that healing, and the container needs to be there 24/7. Our job as teachers is to carry our part during the school day. The parents have the morning, evening, and weekend shift. We are all working together. Mentoring is an opportunity to build a team with a common understanding.

Many of the parents who come to Mulberry Farm have had their children assessed by doctors or psychologists. Many of the prognoses they have been given are dire. Parents have been told their children will never do a long list of things, and those thoughts weigh heavy in hearts. These are things that burn going down. When a family comes to us we begin to take apart those predictions. We get rid of the labels. We constantly see that with the right understanding and within the right setting, those predictions are false. Children whose parents have been told they will never recognize shapes or colors have learned to write and recognize letters and are reading and writing on their own. Children whose parents have been told they have spectrum disorders graduate from Mulberry Farm and move on to regular schools able to participate and learn just like their peers. Children who have been assessed early on and found to be at certain developmental levels surpass the expectations of those assessments. The boy who in fourth grade couldn't count to ten and couldn't recognize letters because his assessments had placed him at the developmental level of a five-year-old is now in ninth grade and able to work with all the math processes you would expect a ninth-grader to know about, including the concepts of beginning algebra. He is now a reader, and he fills his Main Lesson books with his own writing. More importantly, he has found a skill that he really enjoys and one that he is very gifted at. We are working with him to begin to prepare for a career, following his dreams. Parents have been deeply wounded by the things that the "mainstream" has told them about their children. Mentoring is a time to help them heal. The predictions that hurt to hear will hurt again when the parents learn to let go of them. Parents need tender understanding as they relearn to see their child.

Children make rapid progress at Mulberry Farm, and what was true last month is not always true this month. This is another reason for mentoring. Parents need to know that, while it may have been true last month that their child could not tie his or her own shoes, it is not true this month. At school they are tying their shoes. They need to tie them at home as well. This is true for practical skills, and it is also true for behavior. The child who has learned to politely ask for something at school needs to be just as polite at home.

We ask three things of parents at Mulberry. The first is that they eliminate all processed sugar from the children's diet. The second is that the child has no media in his or her life. The third is that the parents come to mentoring and work with the child's teacher so that home life and school life become seamless.

There is one other thing we do to support the parents at

Mulberry Farm. Every year we do a study of Curative Education for the parents and anyone else in the community who might be interested. This gives the parents an opportunity to meet together every month and become a community. When we work together with the pictures of the Curative Polarities we create a common ground for the parents as a group. The parents recognize their own children in these pictures, but they recognize each other's children as well, so no one feels alone. When we work as a group in this way we create a community that can better hold the whole group of children. Parents feel more comfortable sending their children to play with another Mulberry family because they know that they share standards in common.

⋆

Not all children will be able to come to a program like Mulberry Farm. Thinking back to the children in chapter one, although they most likely would all do better if they could be at a program like Mulberry, it may not be possible. So what should that teacher do? Imagine she has now spent time studying Steiner's Curative lectures. Now she has some new ideas. Her classroom looks very different.

The classroom is still a very beautiful space. Nothing there has changed, but something subtle is different. All the children's things are hung neatly on their hooks. Every desk is clutter free and each chair is pushed squarely under the desk. Nothing in the room is out of order. Everything is in good repair. Someone has seen to it that the books are well organized on their shelves. Everywhere you look there is organization and harmony.

The teacher has a different expression on her face. She has worked hard on her own daily rhythm. She comes home on time, she has dinner with her family, and she goes to bed on time. At least once a week she does something that has nothing to do with being a Waldorf teacher. Because she is structuring her lessons differently, putting more of the responsibility of the work onto her students, she needs much less time to prepare. She is no longer bringing students pre-formed, perfect things. The students have to work harder. They like it. They are more engaged and interested in their lessons. This is one of the things that have helped to improve classroom management. Her days are much less difficult, so she is sleeping better. She is striving to work with the Pedagogical Law.

Because she is going to bed on time she is able to get up earlier. She has time for a cup of coffee by herself before the family gets up. She can review her lesson. She has time for a few minutes of morning meditation. Because she is in bed before she is completely worn out she is doing her inner work much more consistently. This is paying off in the classroom. The right ideas are showing up for her. Because the children are now expected to keep the classroom in order the teacher doesn't need to be there quite as early as before. She has time to breathe and live into the picture of the day. She has begun to look forward to the day more than ever before. The knot in her stomach is gone. She still has children who she needs to work harder for, but she feels she has a plan for each of them. She feels she is beginning to meet them and can see them making progress. Her classroom is much more harmonious. All the children are able to do their work in a peaceful setting. The complaints from parents have stopped.

She has met with the parents of the children that have given her the most concerns. They have worked together to make a plan for morning drop-off and afternoon pick-up that works for the children. Other parents no longer get to witness behavior that gives them something to talk about. Recognizing that transition times are so important, the parents of the children who have struggled have organized. The children come to school just as the bell is ringing. They don't have fifteen or twenty minutes of "grey area" time to become anxious and express it in ways that set up their day to be less than successful. Jasper is no longer spinning out in the mornings. His behavior from before was a result of the anxiety he felt. He had become so used to failing in the classroom that he literally couldn't hold himself together. Now he comes right on time. He greets his teacher with confidence. He is being met during Main Lesson, so he no longer fears it.

Sienna's mother has learned to empower her daughter. Instead of asking questions that only feed her child's fear, she now tells her unequivocally every morning that she knows she will have a good day and do really well. When Sienna does complain, her mother listens briefly, but then is careful to tell Sienna that she knows she can solve her difficulties. She brings Sienna back to the present and they enjoy their time at home together more than ever before. The stomach aches and headaches have disappeared.

With the permission of Allen's parents the classroom community has come together to truly support him. If he comes up to someone and begins to perseverate they know now that the kind thing to do is to redirect him. They ask him a question about his weekend, or what he might have done the night before. As a group, the community is helping him to learn about conversations. This loving support has translated into the greater community. He has learned not to approach strangers with lists of facts. When someone asks him a question he can think about it and respond appropriately. Because people have stopped looking at him as if something was a little off, Allen has stopped thinking about himself this way. You can see how much more confident he is.

Max is another one who now arrives promptly. His teacher watches how he approaches the classroom. If he seems to be "out of himself," she asks him to try it again. By bringing him this kind of self-awareness he is much better now at regulating himself.

Alice comes to school with her homework every day now. Her parents have learned to make this her responsibility. For a while this was a hard transition. Alice was used to having people do her thinking for her. She sometimes got really angry when her parents refused to bring her homework into school when she forgot it. Her teacher helped to support the parent's work by making sure she was consequent about Alice's homework. If she forgot it there was a consequence at school. She is now expected to be truly responsible for herself. The result of this is that she has woken up. She has begun to use her own will. Because she is so much more present she is making more friends in the class. She has begun to feel real pride in herself and this is motivating her to more and more progress.

Peter walks up to the classroom all on his own. He knows now he doesn't need help to carry his backpack. He waits his turn in line and shakes his teacher's hand with a new pride in his eyes. He knows how to hang up his own backpack, and settle himself in his desk.

All of these children have already had a short time of walking or running before they come to school. Instead of driving all the way to school, the parents stop about a twenty minute walk away. This has made a huge difference in how the rest of the day has gone. They are also coming to school dressed extra warmly and with layers. Almost every morning this means long sleeves and long pants as well as a warm jacket and hat. This has given each one a little bit more skin. Because they no longer have to work so hard to feel their skin, their behavior has regulated itself. None of them are going to such extremes any more.

Because the rest of the parents in the class are no longer witnessing things in the morning that make them concerned, the attitude toward theses children has shifted. They can see that the children are coming to school much more calmly and ready to work. The parents have become more empathetic and accepting of all the children in the class. Some of them still like to gossip, but none of the families are feeling singled out for attack. None of the children are feeling they have to run the gauntlet to get to their classroom.

Recognizing that all the children in her class need to move each morning, the teacher starts her day by having the children walk and run. She finds it is ten minutes well spent. She has a much better notion of where to begin each day.

She has taken a look at her "morning circle" activities and has begun to include some new material. She takes speech work as an opportunity to include expansion and contraction as gesture. She has replaced the small motor movements that used to frustrate so many of her class with large motor movements that help the children organize themselves better within their own skins. Some days she has the children push their desks together so they can roll over the tops of them. Sometimes, when she feels they need more levity, she has them jump from one row of desks to the next. She has several balance beams in her room of different widths, and when she can see they need more balance they spend some time in the morning working on that. When she does activities involving rhythmic clapping or stepping she pays close attention that each child is really participating. The same goes for activities involving beanbags or juggling balls. When she can see that many of them are not able to follow, she takes the time to take the activity apart, taking smaller steps until each child can succeed. When one or two are still struggling she will make time later in the day to help them one-on-one. The children have begun to trust that all of them are important to her.

She saves music for the end of Main Lesson. She uses it as a breathing out activity leading to snack and recess. When she sees that certain children are not yet able to follow the fine motor skills necessary for a flute or a recorder she finds ways to include them by giving them a rhythmic task for awhile. Many of the children have been really stressed by music, so finding a way that they can succeed helps them to relax and be better able to take up the flute or recorder when they are ready.

Because all of the children are able to do the things being asked of them in morning circle, the distracting behavior tactics of those who weren't able to do things has been greatly reduced. The children are having a much better time because the focus isn't aimed at stopping distracting behavior. Bringing the children some morning movement that involves their whole body has helped make the whole class ready to take up the academic portion of Main Lesson.

The teacher's Main Lesson time has changed quite a lot. There is no more copying off the board. The teacher sees that her job is to bring the children stories, images that the child can live into and then form into narratives on their own. She is the catalyst. She gives them images to begin to work with; the children draw the finished product out of their own selves. At the beginning Main Lesson the class reviews what they have heard about and discussed the day before. They can go back to their composition books and review what they wrote yesterday and see if there is anything they want to add. Before the work goes in their Main Lesson Book, each child comes to the teacher's desk and together they correct the work together. This way the teacher knows just where every student stands in his or her abilities. Each child receives a personal spelling and grammar lesson. She can see trends in the class that tell her when she might want to focus on certain skills with the whole group.

When she tells a new story the children eagerly get to work

with their writing. This is something that each child can be excited about. The work is challenging, but not insurmountable. Jasper is in heaven. For the first time in his life he feels consistently successful. He no longer has the frustration of trying to track words on the board and then maintain the image of them inwardly long enough to copy them into his books. He has a task he can do. He is a very intelligent boy, with a great vocabulary, and he writes things than are interesting to read. His need to "push" has been transformed into a healthy kind of competition with himself. He tries to make each thing he writes a little better than the day before. He has been asked to read some of his compositions out loud to the class, and this is beginning to heal the shame he felt when he made such a mess of his work trying to copy. He knows he still needs to work on his handwriting, but his great success in content has allowed him to be much more willing to try than before. Because he is feeling success for the first time in his life his behavior has improved dramatically. He still needs clear boundaries. When he pushes with his actions he needs to feel the teacher is holding him with the inner strength that makes him feel secure. There are still bumps during the day in special subject classes. When Jasper feels the task is too great for him he will still act out as subterfuge. The teacher is doing her best to speak with the faculty about what she has found works with Jasper. He trusts her more now, and tries to do his best all day so that he can please her.

The teacher has moved Sienna to the back of the room. Having no one in her backspace has helped her to relax much more. She no longer feels scrutinized by the entire class. From the back of the room she has a vantage point where she can observe the class calmly. She is beginning to risk raising her hand when she is certain about an answer. When she has difficulty starting something the teacher helps her by giving her one small step after another to complete. She recognizes the "deer in the headlights" look when it shows up in Sienna's eyes. The teacher stays calm. She doesn't reflect the fear she sees in the child. She holds inwardly the strong belief that Sienna can do it. She may start by just asking Sienna to get out her composition book and her pencil. As soon as she has done that she tells Sienna to come see her. At her desk she might ask Sienna to tell her something she remembers from the story. When Sienna does, she tells her to go write just that in her book. Sometimes Sienna will say she doesn't know how to spell all the words. The teacher tells her that's OK. Just sound them out the best you can. We'll fix it later. Most often, when Sienna has been able to make a start with a sentence or two, the rest of her work will flow much more freely. She feels that her teacher believes in her and this gives her the courage to believe in herself.

Peter no longer has an aid. He is expected to do many things by himself now. No one is fetching his supplies or clearing up after him later. When there is something he does need help with the teacher asks another child to work with him. Without the aid around Peter the children feel much more open and willing to approach. He is no longer in a bubble where the children can't connect to him. The teacher had to start with very small steps with Peter. He was not used to listening during stories or lessons, because he never had to be responsible for their content before. He may have put some things from the board in his book, but he never gave thought to what he was doing. He may have formed letters, but he never formed a relationship to the letters. The first step for him is teaching him he needs to listen to the story. He is more than capable of this, but as no one has ever expected it of him he has never thought to do it. Now the teacher asks him every day to tell her something from the day's lesson. He has gotten very good at this. She asks him to draw something from the story in his Main Lesson book. This is a start. There are times he seems to freeze up and the teacher can see that, although he knows what to do, he cannot seem to get his body to cooperate. When she sees this, the teacher will call out his name brightly. She will give him a warm smile. This acts as a little jump-start that will get Peter going again. Sometimes he gets frustrated because he doesn't know how to draw the thing. When she sees that there is a child who has finished the day's work, she might ask that child to give Peter some ideas. She makes it clear that the child should not do Peter's work for him, but the child can help by breaking down the drawing into smaller steps, and Peter learns by watching. The next step will be to get Peter to try to write some words from the story. There are some letters that Peter is still fuzzy about. He is no longer in first grade, so drawing the letter out of a fairy tale is no longer appropriate, but there is always something in the stories the class is hearing now that can be used instead. Step-by-step, Peter can begin to move forward. He is much more involved with the class now. He goes home and tells his parents about what he has heard at school for the first time ever. The children can see how hard he is working and they have come to respect him for his efforts. Every day they are finding more and more ways to involve him in their activities.

The teacher has helped Max by giving him clear parameters about his work. He has a plethora of ideas, but his will is still untamed, so he struggles to complete things. To help Max the teacher tells him he needs to write just one good sentence a day. The sentence must be clear. The content must be accurate. Nothing that wasn't talked about in the lesson may be included in the sentence. This is teaching Max to discipline his thinking. The sentence must be written neatly in his Main Lesson Book, and the drawing he does for it must be complete. Again, it may not contain space aliens or implements of war or anything that wasn't part of the story. Soon Max will be able to write a correct sentence consistently. Then he will be asked to write a paragraph. He will work up to a full composition. When Max has successfully accomplished the day's task he has a window box project he can work on. In it he is creating a beeswax world from some element of the year's curriculum. This gives him an outlet for his vast imagination. The only stipulation is that the box has to stay true to the content he has chosen. Again, no ninja warriors or vampires if he's chosen ancient Egypt as his scenario. The teacher makes sure that before each transition time in the class she brings the group to stillness. This medicine particularly serves Max. Because he is given the opportunity to completely breath in during these transition times he never goes so far out. This has helped create more order and calm in the classroom, and all of the children benefit from that.

The teacher's work with Allen is similar to the work with Max, and a little like the work with Peter as well. She also asks Allen to write her just one good sentence. She helps him to begin by calling him to her desk and asking him to recall something from the lesson.

In the beginning this was very hard for him, but as he began to feel that the teacher was patient and supportive of him, he began to try. At first he could only bring out fragments of ideas. The teacher worked with him to shape the fragments into full thoughts that were sentences. He is beginning to have a feeling for a thought that is complete. When Allen finishes his work for the day he has a special knitting project in his desk that he can take out and work on. Knitting takes his propensity towards repetition and gives it an appropriate framework. When he knits he is creating something he can share with others. Each member of his family now has a scarf made by Allen. He takes care to think of each one, choosing colors and patterns he thinks they will like. Often the teacher asks him to sit by her during snack or lunch. They practice having conversations. Sometimes the children don't know what to make of Allen, but they have begun to notice that he is not the same as he used to be. They notice he is progressing. He hardly ever repeats the same story over and over again. When the teacher hears him repeat something, like the cat story, she approaches him very calmly and quietly and whispers to him, "We are done with that now. We can let that go." Some of the children are working to connect with him and involve him in games at recess. Allen is smiling for the first time ever.

The work that Alice's parents and her teacher have begun, helping her to be more accountable, continues all day at school. Each day the teacher sets Alice a reasonable goal. This amount must be completed each day. If not, there is a consequence. It may mean she spends part of her recess working, or takes the work home for homework. The teacher has been very careful to only give Alice tasks she knows she can accomplish. This kind of consistent expectation of accountability has taken root in Alice. Very rarely is her work not complete at the end of Main Lesson. The teacher has also given Alice the task of leading the rest of the class in Morning Verse. This means Alice is participating in it for the first time ever. This kind of rhythmical repetition has also been good "medicine" for her sulphur qualities.

During the time that the children are working independently the teacher stays put at her desk. Because her back is never turned from the children there is never the opportunity to do things behind her back. Because the children have work to do that satisfies them they are able now to work calmly. The only sound you hear is the humming of happy workers.

Although there will always be areas where the teacher wishes she could improve, or things she feels she doesn't know enough about, she has now come to a place where she feels confident she is seeing each child in her care in a better light. She has more understanding and more tools to work with. She sees each one as an individual, not as a set of mysterious difficulties she's not trained to handle. She too can go home each day feeling she has done her best. When she begins to feel she might be losing her way she remembers to say to herself inwardly, "I can do it!"

In this stage of regenerating we are working with the highest capacities of our own will. We are not copying what Steiner or anyone else may have done before us—we are making the work new everyday. Steiner may have given us the framework, but what we do within that framework is our own work. We are not working unconsciously, mindlessly repeating what has been done before— we are giving birth to something that is distinctly ours. This is the last stage of the seven life processes. It is the "motive" of our free will rising beyond what we might feel "compelled" to do. If we have allowed our soul to follow along the path of the seven life processes at a rate it can follow, if we have allowed all that we are trying to learn to ripen in our hearts at the right tempo, then we have come to this place where we can regenerate out of our own free will and consciousness. Hopefully, we can look around us and see the deeds of will that have created our own work as curative educators. We have been following a path, and for the moment we have reached a summit. We can stop here for now and enjoy the view.

BIBLIOGRAPHY

Aeppli, Willi. *The Care and Development of the Human Senses* (Edinburgh: Floris Books, 2013).

Bort, Julia, Walter Holtzapfel and Hermann Kirchner. *Heilende Erziehung* (Stuttgart: Verlag Freies Geistesleben, 1998).

Groh, Irene and Mona Ruef. *Erzeihung und Unterricht Als Praeventivmedizin* (Dornach: Medizinishe Sektion am Goetheanum, 2002).

König, Karl. *Die Ersten drei jahre des Kindes* (Stuttgart: Verlag Freies Geistesleben, 1963).

König, Karl. *Embryologie und Weltenstehung* (Schaffhausen: Novalis Verlag, 1986).

König, Karl. *Heilpaedagogishche Diagnostik* (Arlesheim: Natura Verlag, 1983/1984).

König, Karl. *The Human Soul* (Spring Valley: Anthroposophic Press, 1973.)

König, Karl. *A Living Physiology* (n.p.: Camphill Books, 1999).

König, Karl. *Der Kries der zwoelf Sinne und die sieben Lebensprozesse* (Stuttgart: Verlag Freies Geistesleben, 1999).

König, Karl. *Sinnesentwicklung und Leiberrfahrung* (Stuttgart: Verlag Freies Geistesleben, 1971).

König, Karl. *Vortraege zum Heilpadagogischen Kurs Rudolf Steiners* (Stuttgart: Verlag Freies Geistesleben, 2000).

Lehrs, Ernst. *Von Geist der Sinne* (Frankfurt am Main: Klostermann, 1994).

Lievegoed, Prof. Dr. B.C.J. *Heilpaedagogische Betractungen* (Zeist: Christofoor, 1952).

Presses, Simeon. *Bewegung ist Heilung* (Stuttgart: Verlag Freies
    Geistesleben, 1984).

Selg, Peter. *The Therapeutic Eye: How Rudolf Steiner Observed Children*
    (Great Barrington, MA: SteinerBooks, 2008).

Soesman, Albert. *Our Twelve Senses* (Stroud: Hawthorn Press, 1999).

Steiner, Rudolf. *Anthroposophy (A Fragment)* (Hudson, NY: Anthropo-
    sophic Press, 1996).

Steiner, Rudolf. *Autobiography: Chapters in the Course of My Life* (Great
    Barrington, MA: SteinerBooks, 2005).

Steiner, Rudolf. *Curative Education* (London: Rudolf Steiner Press,
    1972).

Steiner, Rudolf. *Die zwoelf Sinne des Menchen in irher Beziehung zu
    Imagination, Inspiration, Intuition* (Dornach: Verlag Der Rudolf
    Steiner, 1967).

Weihs, Thomas J. *Das entwicklungsgestoerte Kind* (Stuttgart: Verlag
    Freies Geistesleben, 1974).